# COLD WAR II
## A GUIDE TO WHAT WE CAN DO;
## NOT A EULOGY

## LAYLA FARIDANI

*For the victims*

FOR THE CRIMINALS:

آن قصر که جمشید در او جام گرفت

آهو بچه کرد و روبه آرام گرفت

بهرام که گور میگرفتی همه عمر

دیدی که چگونه گور بهرام گرفت

The palace where Jamshid raised a glass
Where the deer and the fox pass
    Bahram who hunted with grave
See how the grave hunted Bahram
            -Omar Khayyam

(calligraphy by Seyed Faridani)

# TABLE OF CONTENTS

# OUR MONEY

In the summer of 2019, the media was covering the situation at detention centers down at the southern border. They constantly showed images of large populations of immigrants being lined up in small spaces and repeated the fact that children are being separated from their parents. After this came the lack of food and health supplies. CNN in particular maximized the volume when reporting on the fact that even donations cannot be accepted to support the immigrants.

After that summer, suddenly there was no more talk of how detention centers were doing. No more talk of children crying for their parents. No more talk of the cruelty of piling up masses of people in small spaces. Had the arrests ended? Was there a stop to detention camps? Had they been shut down?

No. After the emotional news, the media was able to pass a $4 billion budget in Congress to care for the camps and provide food and sanitary needs. Illegal immigrants continued to be locked up and children continued to cry. The event was not a one-time crisis. It was not a single incident in which degradation of human beings occurred. The arrest and transfer of illegal immigrants to detention centers is a non-stop around the clock activity funded by taxpayer money.

In his book, *Beyond These Walls*, Tony Platt deeply covers the secrets, schemes and darkness of the prison industry. He mentions how every day 14 million Americans are stopped for minor violations but really those minor violations such as a traffic law are used as a pretext to arrest people on some other major violation like drug possession. In America, 65 million people have a criminal record yet could all them be rightfully called criminals? The privatization of prisons has taken the biggest toll. Private prisons are known to be more chaotic, more corrupt, and more massive in size. Labeling theory has also played a role in such a way that Muslims and black people are automatically considered or suspected to be criminal or as Platt would like to say "criminogenic: inherently abnormal and predestined to crime." The book is probably the most insightful when it comes to researching the prison system and its many flaws. Platt labels Native American reservations, Nazi concentration camps, American prisons, Palestine and European refugee camps as Centers for Dehumanization. Here different groups reside under harsh conditions that impose degradation, cruelty and oppression. I would add pornography studios to his list. Nazi camps may have come to an end yet the model is multiplying to different settings. People witness neglect, alienation and oppression on a daily basis yet neoliberals would rather label them as women having every right to do anything they want to their own bodies, or immigrant rights. They call for propping up the Centers for Dehumanization rather than shutting them down. Palestinians witness their homes being crushed by European settlers. Native Americans lack drinking water. The European Union demands transit countries such as Turkey pile up migrants in order to prevent them from reaching Europe. These events are based on organizational culture and the shared belief system among these facilities that gives the prison guards or higher officials the right to treat humans with such humiliation.

I do not want to go over the entire process but all these shameful acts by law enforcement and agencies is costing us a lot. Not to mention our prisons outside of the country like Bagram and the all too famous Guantanamo which so far three presidents have promised to shut down. Their aim in construction was for housing American terrorists and to prevent them from returning to their homeland. We like to pretend radicalization happens outside and is imported to our country. Platt goes over what happens when beds are not used, cells are empty, and services go unneeded. If detention centers are not filled with illegal immigrants the government is forced to pay a fine. Therefore, we have a middle situation where immigrants are not being sent back and they are not being allowed into the country. That middle situation is called the prison industry.

It has been estimated that the American presence in Syria and Iraq has cost our government over $1 billion. This is aside from the official budget we put toward our military and personnel. This amount was dedicated to the various groups the Central Intelligence Agency had put together to overthrow yet another foreign leader; this time President Assad of Syria. I was 16 when I started taking notes on the so-called "Arab Spring" which turned out to be nothing more than a series of coups promoted by our media. Masses of people young and old left their homes, businesses and memories. They were oppressed and became victims of cruelty. Many aimed for the European Union countries to give them back what they had taken away from them. Prisoners escaped, museums were looted, and cultural heritage was destroyed by ISIS, Al-Nusra and the Free Syrian Army. The groups' mission was to solely create chaos and fear. They did not care about who was in power or what would happen after Assad's ouster. They carried no flag. When CNN and even the New York Times and Wall Street Journal claimed President Assad "killed his own people" President Obama was urged to do something. I have three notebooks filled with notes since 2011 on not just Syria and Iraq but the whole chaos and commotion our money was able to fund across the regions of West Asia and North Africa. Neoliberals made sure the photos of Aylan Kurdi on the shores of Turkey were publicized everywhere in order to sell us another humanitarian war while they censored the liberation of Aleppo a few years later. According to the CIA, whenever populations are in trouble it is our mission to quickly put together numerous groups and send them to save the day. Yet we were not alone in the funding and training. Our allies that have always been by our side were committed to opening their borders to anyone who wanted to join ISIS, Al- Nusra, the Free Syrian Army and many more smaller affiliates. They too sent their armies and intelligence to work and called for the removal of President Assad. As of today the operation has failed thanks to Syria's army, Iran and Russia. Refugees who have fled are starting to return back home.

As the process continued over the decade it turned out that removing Bashar Assad was not the only goal of the CIA and that our money was also being spent toward something else. Something that did not get Congressional approval when the major budget was laid out. In Iraq, there were calls for the division of Kurdistan. Many Kurdish organizations were also gathered by the CIA to hit two birds with a single stone. And of course way before that we were "guarding the oil" as President Trump would like to call it.

The CIA has also long called for the overthrow of Venezuelan president Nicholas Maduro. It has called life in Venezuela a "humanitarian crisis" and many people have left the country due to economic struggles. Through the United States Aid for International Development we have sent loads and loads of humanitarian packages down to the country containing food and water. The news surrounding Venezuela has significantly impacted how Americans view this oil rich nation. They show sympathy and emotion; however, Venezuela is not a poor nation. It has just as much oil as Saudi Arabia but it has been barred from export. Supermarkets are packed with meat, dairy and grains. While the sanctions have caused high inflation and expense, citizens claim it is not that there is a lack of food in the country but rather the products and groceries have become outrageously expensive. They simply cannot buy what is in fact present in the stores because they do not have the money. During one process of shipment from America to Venezuela our government claimed President Maduro had burnt humanitarian aid. The scene of flames had been caught twice by reporters and what they found was shameful. Masked men were identified burning the shipments in one scene

4

while the same men were caught burning another shipment in another scene.

The CIA has also been caught with assassination attempts and terrorizing President Maduro. In fact, the CIA has indirectly assassinated many world leaders: Hosni Mubarak of Egypt; Mohammadreza Pahlavi of Iran; Mohammad Morsi of Egypt; and Reza Pahlavi of Iran. Morsi was our first choice before Abdel Fattah Al-Sisi, yet when it was made clear he did not side with American interests he was immediately removed through a second coup. Morsi and Mubarak both spent years in prison where they were neglected by authorities and eventually lost their lives due to poor health services. Mubarak had been to court numerous times on a hospital bed and was so ill he had to be released from prison. The Pahlavi's probably had it the worst. Unlike Mubarak and Morsi, the father and son were exiled from their own country and sent to unknown lands. The son commonly known as the Shah is currently buried in Egypt where he lost his life to cancer. *Shah* means king in Persian. Reza Shah on the other hand is buried in Tehran; however, he too suffered from health-related reasons. The cruelty does not stop there. Two of the Shah's children committed suicide after leaving all their power, wealth, rank and popularity in Iran and moving to America.

When many Americans had just lost their homes to fake loans and money borrowed from big banks such as Wells Fargo, President Obama was busy overthrowing the president of Honduras. Americans were homeless and many still are due to the fall of the housing market yet the country's top priority at the moment was to send President Zelaya to Costa Rica and make sure he remains there. The Honduran Supreme Court was on our side and helped kick out the president who was providing free lunch meals to students, working toward green energy, giving pensions to seniors and building new infrastructure.

In his book *Gullible Superpower*, Ted Carpenter goes over a long list of coups from the 1950s on to the 2010s. Every chapter is dedicated to a world leader who was removed from power (or an attempt was made) ranging from Mohammad Mossadegh all the way to Bashar Assad. The book is a must read if you have not been following developments in Syria, Honduras or Venezuela. After every coup came decades of chaos, poverty and migration. If we are promoting democracy and justice then why are people fleeing their homes? What is sad is that the citizens of those countries were not alone in the suffering. When the North Atlantic Treaty Organization (NATO) was busy protecting terrorists in Libya from Moammar Ghadafi's airstrikes, 125,128 people in California were homeless; 18% of Spanish students left high school; and the wars in Afghanistan and Iraq were still ongoing. Americans were suffering in various ways that did not matter to those above because they were more concerned with removing a "dictator" and bringing democracy and freedom to the world. Carpenter also lists the most thuggish groups we sponsored in order to get rid of leaders deemed undesirable. The Mojahedin, UNITA, Mojahedin Khalgh, Kosovo Liberation Army and the Contras are just some of the groups the CIA put together to promote the coups. Similarly, Al-Nusra and the Free Syrian Army were committed to theft and spreading cruelty and oppression. Their sheer ignorance toward the leaders and the citizens was shown when terrorists in Libya also attacked the American consulate in Benghazi. Our ambassador Christopher Stevens died in the process and no one on the American side was held accountable. In fact, the situation in Libya became so embarrassing that CNN, The New York Times, The Washington Post and other news outlets that promoted the Arab Spring basically gave up reporting on Libya.

When the Taliban took over Afghanistan, President George H.W. Bush gifted Osama bin Laden with the title of "freedom fighter." If these groups were committed to freedom, then why did they kill and destroy everyone and everything that came their way regardless of whose side they were on? Millions of Afghans have fled their country and are seeking refuge in neighboring Iran and Pakistan. During all of this funding Americans were feeling abandoned, neglected, disaffected, and ignored. They found less and less meaning in voting and the democratic process. They got their hopes up when the first black president came to power or when more troops started coming back home, but the moment did not last.

Of course, there have been instances where violence was limited. This only occurs when the CIA is able to find a coup leader who would eventually lead the country after the so-called "dictator's" departure. A few good examples would be Juan Guaido for Venezuela and Abdel Fattah Al-Sisi for Egypt. When we observe the coup process in these countries we see that less violence and terror exists and people live in a more calm setting after the coup compared to when the CIA is left with no replacement for the departed leader. Many of us ask why have we spent 19 years in Afghanistan? A country with no oil or any other natural resources, no water, and lots of heroin. This is because the CIA has been struggling to find a reliable leader for Afghanistan. Hamed Karzai has proven to be incompetent and unreliable while our military has spent much on funding him and his government. We are still relying on terrorist organizations to run the country and take on leadership.

Take a look at Libya, Egypt's next door neighbor. Why is Libya run by a terrorist organization known as the National Transitional Council while Egypt is run by a military general? How come there is less chaos in Egypt after Hosni Mubarak's departure while Libyans live with slavery and terrorism after Ghadafi (two things that did not exist under Ghadafi's rule)? This is because Egypt had a coup leader while Libya lacked a plan B. The chaos ended once Abdel Fattah Al-Sisi took power, yet in Libya there was no one hand-picked to lead the country after Ghadafi. As of now, the CIA is still searching.

The chaos and violence we funded in Iraq, Syria, Libya, Algeria, Egypt, Serbia, Sudan, Iran, Afghanistan, Yemen and Tunisia took place in the same way right here in the USA. Karma. The elites thought they could escape the horrors they bring to other people and that whatever happens could never reach American territory. That chaos is easy to provoke in far off lands where the leaders are hated, and the citizens are poor. However, among the peaceful protesters who were coming out against dehumanization and racism in Minnesota, were the same type of thugs who overthrew Ghadafi, Mubarak, Saleh and others. They did not carry a flag and were not interested in what would happen after George Floyd's unjustified death. The thugs burnt down supermarkets and businesses. They looted the stores the same way thugs looted museums in Egypt. Minnesota became a scene from Tahrir Square in Egypt where smoke rose up into the blue sky and government officials scrambled to control their own people. Chaos erupted in the middle of protests where people just wanted to make a stand and defend humanity. When the CIA was degrading people in Iraq and Syria in 2015, our police force was degrading Freddie Gray in Maryland. While the elites enjoyed violence in these two countries they were not so satisfied by the scenes in America. CNN and many other news channels censored the scenes of violence and only captured images of peaceful protesters who were gathered around and were making chants against racism. Yet when thugs divided Ghadafi's body in half and put him on display the media was rooting for them and congratulating them for toppling their leader. Terrorists in Libya, Egypt and Tunisia were labeled freedom fighters while the same type of people in Missouri, Maryland, Indiana and many other states were labeled thugs. The media supported Gray, Floyd and Martin while at the same time defending the very elites who sponsored their death just like they sponsored the CIA's schemes in West Asia and North Africa while claiming to defend their citizens. They did not blame the neoliberal agenda and missed the bigger picture about justice under globalism. Humans are not inherently good when left unchecked and free to decide everything on their own. The media solely took this as a racist event and ignored elite culture and views on various groups in America and abroad. That these groups are less than human and that it is okay to abuse them. Police brutality against African-Americans became another opportunity for the elites to profit off of the human rights industry; another never ending war.

It amazes me that when it comes to exporting democracy we have so many resources; so many sponsors and so much funding available. Yet when it comes to providing health care we suddenly get reminded of the debt. Next to the cash we also have so much sympathy, emotions, and humanitarianism. What happened to all that emotion when we saw millions of Americans go homeless over-night after the housing market fell? How come no lobbyist has ever come out for them and supported their cause? Where is the Aylan Kurdi of 2008? How come his pictures did not go viral and catch anyone's emotions? My guess is because there had been no one to demonize but the banks, therefore, the elites refrained from blaming anyone at all.

Many traditionalists have been criticizing President Trump's view of where American money has been going since the end of the first Cold War. They believe our money should go toward healing the poor of the world; international institutions; the "war on terror" and of course populations begging for democracy and justice. Since his time in office Trump has cut all of these efforts and believes these are nothing but expenses. On foreign aid, he cut money toward Pakistan. On global missions, he defunded the United Nations Educational, Scientific & Cultural Organization (UNESCO) and the World Health Organization (WHO). His actions have brought anger and fear not just for Americans but also the world population.

Perhaps his actions are questionable but we as Americans can remember times when our money was spent in ways that were just as beneficial and good for humanity and definitely not wasted. The Social Security Act was one of these programs. It is cherished by most Americans and probably the best thing the government has ever done to help the lives of the elderly. The G.I. bill was created to sponsor education for veterans who would come back from war with no fu-ture. The Violent Crime Control & Law Enforcement Act of 1994, which brought a ten year ban on assault rifles, many of which were used in the recent spree of mass shootings. These are just some of the great things tax money was able to accomplish and can be aligned with the mission of the WHO, as well as with missions geared toward fighting terror.

In my recent trip to Toronto, I was able to visit another Western nation which turned out to be dealing with some of the most pressing issues we face in America. I was able to compare and contrast the struggles and notice a lot about the city. Rick Steves calls this "travel as a political act." The all-time traveler's host of *Rick Steve's Europe* says when we decide to visit another country, another state or even another town we should not just look for malls and restaurants. We should not just take a tan at the beach or look for duty free. We must examine the people of the region; the buildings; the struggles and the daily life experience of the residents. Toronto is friendly, relaxed and surprisingly not loud or overpopulated, which is not what you would expect from a city. C.N. Tower is one of the main attractions and surely a symbol of Toronto. When I visited there with my family I noticed the large immigrant population waiting to enter the aquarium with excitement and eagerness. Immigrants in Canada are definitely integrated and not alienated from the rest of the population. However, what I also noticed next to that was the absence of the white population. I thought this is C.N. Tower, a tourist area built in 1976 that cannot necessarily be qualified as new infrastructure yet it is not segregated either. Why would white people not be interested in visiting? This phenomenon reminded me of how Canada, similar to America, is a nation of immigrants. It may be hard to come down to the things people share but we must identify some infrastructure, some foods, sports and holidays in order to prevent alienation and loss of hope.

Christmas and New Year's in Toronto are just as big as in New York. People were gathered in Dundas Avenue with all the lights and advertisement shining in their eyes as if it were Times Square. While there I noticed the homeless. They were no different than the homeless in American cities. Some asked for help while others just sat looking at the people having a good time and taking photos. What turned out to be disturbing was the fact that most homeless in Toronto were also not in a good mental state. They seemed to be in their own worlds while walking up and down a street right next to a popular hotel. We decided to take the subway and again there were homeless men who were not in a very good mental state. As we walked down Dundas we could not help but notice the heavy smell of marijuana rushing past people as they enjoyed their time. Marijuana is legal under Canadian law and no one is arrested for its possession. There are legal facilities set up in Toronto for people to enter and privately use the drug. We passed by one of them and there was a long line of young people waiting to be admitted entry by the security guard. Although the rules and regulations concerning marijuana in Canada were impressive, I wished that I had seen those people who were waiting in line, waiting to enter C.N. Tower.

After visiting the tower, we stayed at my cousin's house and we were introduced to her new children. Her husband was talking about the great opportunities Canada has as far as jobs go and that having a barbecue at the end of the week is still a thing in that country. This had me comparing American weekends: full-time work, no one to care for the children and definitely no more barbecues. Sundays once were dedicated to religious duties and the church. Now employers put their workers on schedule without regard to religious rights even if they are not church-goers.

On our last day we headed toward Niagara Falls. The area reminded me of our own Vegas; all the casinos were busy; restaurants were fancy and of course hotels were abundant. It's really a beautiful sight when the water connects the two countries in a way that Canada is on one side and America is on the other. At the waterfall I witnessed the same scene I had witnessed at C.N. Tower: immigrants with their parents, children, spouses and pets but no sign of white people. With all the fear the media likes to create about travel abroad and the demonization of certain countries our drive to Toronto was not challenged at all. We were easily able to enter the country and leave without any fear of the topics CNN and the other networks constantly feed to our brains on a daily basis. We did not hesitate to go into large gatherings nor did we avoid people wearing the *hijab* and other features we have been told are associated with terrorism. Perhaps there are more legitimate fears when we leave our people in the streets. When we have them searching for what could make them feel part of something. When we cut them off from anything that has to do with family and togetherness. Perhaps we should fear what is tangible; not invisible.

# OUR ENVIRONMENT

R.I. International is a worldwide organization dedicated to four topics: crisis, health, recovery and consulting. They promote suicide prevention, rehabilitation, peer recovery and counseling through 50 programs all over America and abroad.

In their May 2019 interview with a Peer Support Specialist named Charlie the organization reveals how environmental factors lead to people taking drugs for an answer to their pains. Charlie mentions that he was abused by his parents as a child. This was what put him on the wrong path. He says he eventually looked to biker clubs as a source of protection. Later he would marry, divorce and remarry multiple times. He describes himself as "having a Ph.D. from the streets" but after a few years in prison he finally came to recovery classes only to find his way in life and become a specialist himself. The experience has transformed his world view and connected him to things that give him responsibility, leadership, power and self-worth once more. He gets emotional when talking about being able to find work for an elderly woman who wanted to leave the nursing home and become independent. Seeing her every day on the job made Charlie feel a "sense of purpose" and a role to play in this world. Before he entered his life of alienation, Charlie was receiving purpose and belonging from his family until that disappeared. What he recommends toward the end of the video is for people to give away part of themselves for someone who is more needy and weaker than they are. This was his solution for those who share his past.

Charlie's story and experience made me wonder how many youth are in trouble today. If the solution is to be more compassionate and caring, then why did President Obama dedicate $500 million toward mental health awareness in 2012 after the Connecticut school shooting? More disturbing, why did we have shootings repeat back to back throughout the 2010s after that major budget? Can it not be possible that at least one of those young men who committed such horrific attacks share the same story as Charlie?

*The Independent* published a story in November 2016 regarding the real reason behind youth joining terrorist groups. This was when ISIS and their ilk were at their height and our media was reporting on the attacks in Paris and Brussels in a non-stop fashion. It was titled "ISIS: Islam is not Strongest Factor Behind Foreign Fighters Joining Extremist Groups in Syria and Iraq-Report." The article focuses on some eye-catching information by West Point and their Combating Terrorism Center for which they conducted a series of studies in order to find out that most of the young men who are attracted to ISIS have in fact no clear knowledge of Islam at all and have never had any religious studies in their entire lives. Some former radicals who had returned to their native countries were surveyed by West Point and reported having "basic" knowledge of Islam and therefore, did some research before becoming members. They used *The Koran for Dummies* and *Islam for Dummies*. They did not even look to their local mosque for guidance but rather were recruited by online propaganda or their friends. The C.T.C. also looked into the background of these terrorists and found that most were unemployed or were students living in immigrant communities isolated from the white populations of France, Germany, Belgium and Britain.

*The Los Angeles Times* published a rare story on the life and childhood of Rizwan Farook, the San Bernardino, California terrorist. It mentioned how Farook's father abused his family just a few years before Farook did what he did. He was unemployed, an alcoholic and constantly in an angry mood around his family. One time he threw a TV set on Farook's mother. His mother on the other hand was a full-time secretary at a medical facility. Since her husband was not working she had to pay for the family and work full-time. Farook's parents once filed for divorce but his mother rescinded her request. The violence continued. His mother says Farook and her other children were always in the middle of saving their mother from some kind of violence by their father. Farook and his siblings always witnessed fear and harm in their family. A few years later, Farook and his wife entered into a social services building in California and shot 14 people dead.

The explosion at Murrah Federal Building in Oklahoma City in 1995 was a devastating event in American history. Over 160 people died and many were injured. The terrorist was Timothy McVeigh, an intelligent college drop-out and veteran of the Persian Gulf War. McVeigh's parents separated when he was young and his mother and sisters moved from New York all the way down to Florida. He was raised solely by his father. McVeigh's grandfather introduced him to guns and took him to shooting ranges. As he got older he found an attachment to guns and felt gun rights were being violated by the government. The Branch Davidians, a Christian religious community, was a point of interest for him. He was 29 when he broke out.

Patrick Crusius was a recent college graduate and the son of divorced parents. His father had been married before and broke up his first family before being remarried. He was addicted to various drugs all throughout his life and this impacted Crusius's environment in such a way that Crusius's mother left the family. In 2019, Crusius drove to a Walmart store in Texas and shot mostly Mexican shoppers to death. This was before he posted hate messages online even though he had no prior record of racism or a racist confrontation with any non-white person in his life. However, the media focused less on his disturbed life and more on his recent post online. They claimed Crusius was a racist and right-winger who found some way to vent his frustration through terror. In fact, Crusius was never identified with any right-wing terror organization or group. The high school he attended had 20% Spanish students.

Johann Hari is a Swiss-Brit journalist with a focus on addiction and environmental issues surrounding the human life. His family was heavily affected by drugs and various social issues before he was old enough to understand. In his 2015 TED talk show he introduces an experiment questioning what the public really knows about various addictions, from mainstream drugs to video gaming to shopping to the internet.

The experiment involved a rat living in its cage. It was given water to drink but also a mix of water and heroin. The rat never obsessed over the plain water but constantly used the water and heroin mix. The outcome was no surprise until the scientists added a few toys, a wheel and a rat friend to the cage. Hari mentions how the rats rarely went toward the heroin and were mostly busy playing or eating and using all the new features the scientists had added. Neither of them lost their lives and neither of them overdosed.

Hari says this is not just limited to animals and can be applied to humans. He brings up the example of Vietnam veterans and how they used drugs when on the war scene. Remarkably, once the war ended and the soldiers returned home, 95% of them abandoned drugs without going through rehabilitation. They simply put it away when their environment went from violent to calm.

When I was a child I remember watching Animal Planet a lot with my brother. The TV channel used to actually show animals instead of "Finding Bigfoot" or "I Shouldn't Be Alive." One show we watched was "Animal Cops" and it was about how the

A.S.P.C.A. and other authorities would confiscate pets and wild animals people had hoarded in their homes. Everything from snakes, rats, monkeys to dogs and cats were hidden inside the homes. The people would get arrested for neglect and mismanagement of their so-called pets while the animals themselves would be taken away to a humane society or shelter. Dogs were skinny, urine was all over the floor, and odor ran through the windows. At that time I did not think these people were missing something in their lives. I did not even pay attention to the fact that most of the residents were living alone. Now that I reflect, I can see these people were searching for substitutes. They had nothing to give them hope and meaning. Nothing to provide a sense of belonging. They had a story of abuse, abandonment and violence. They felt alienated. Every time they would bring in a new animal to, for instance, replace their parents and their love but it would not satisfy them so they would bring in another animal; this time a wild one. Before they realized it, they were running a zoo in their neighborhood and the police were at their door. The people would cry when the cops were caging what was supposed to give them meaning and make them feel a part of something. It was a sad scene but in reality it was not just the pets that were being saved; it was also the people.

Hari prefers to call addiction "bonding." He emphasizes work, family, connections, responsibilities, parenting and the things that need to be in our "cage" in order to prevent us from ever needing something as dangerous as heroin or less harmful like hoarding pets. If I were in charge of all the human rights organizations; charities; private and public institutions; health care programs; churches and counseling advocates I would abandon all missions and simply focus all donations, volunteers and budget toward saving things that give us purpose. All these walkathons, various events and fundraisers are great and definitely effective for awareness, yet they do not tackle the main causes of alienation. They are either late when the damage has already been done and for example, a young woman is homeless with a child or they are focused on a particular phenomenon. For example, I see green bags or T-shirts that have "End Suicide" written on them or the green ribbon in memory of the Connecticut school shooting. These are not bad ideas but how does "End Suicide" help us understand why people lose hope and experience alienation? People taking their own lives does not mean they should have used more medication or took therapy sessions. Shootings and terrorism does not mean we have a gun issue. These are only the result of people's environment. It means the people who committed these crimes felt disconnected, powerless and alienated. Imagine all Non Profit Organizations abandoning their work and instead working to fund programs that are meant to keep families together; provide jobs for youth; educate the teenagers who left high school and their teachers never even offered to home school them; introduce reliable friends to lonely individuals who distance themselves from society; give responsibility to young men who feel there is no hope and they are not needed in their own community. Even programs like "Walk to End Alzheimer's" can save the family, work, connections, friends and traditions. I think such a wonderful alliance would impact society in such a way that less shootings would occur; less suicide would happen; less drugs would be used; radical groups like Al-Qaeda and the Alt-Right would lose members; less shopping would happen; less time would be spent on video games; and all people regardless of whether they were living in an empty cage or not would be safer and calm.

No one will be safe if even one person is in pain. There is really no difference between gangs, drugs, terrorist organizations, shopping, video games… when we see that these only pop into our lives when we have nothing to do or in the words of Hari when our cage is empty. Their purpose is the same. Many police investigations are focused on a suspect's background and personal traits such as Asian or white; immigrant or American; Muslim or

Christian; and mentally disturbed or healthy. These personal char-acteristics say nothing about unemployment, isolation, crisis or loss of connections. They do not relate to any of the common de-nominators I found among all the terrorists regardless of whether they were immigrants, white or Asian, Muslim or non-Muslim or mentally disabled or sane. Investigators are not relying on evidence based practices. Their research on various cases goes against the facts of the crime. Being Muslim does not increase your chances of walking into a public area and shooting random people to death. Being racist does not give you the ability to put your thoughts about various groups into action and shoot them to death. Coming from a failing family does. The result of all these misinterpreta-tions has been more tax money going toward programs that do not support the causes of young men lashing out. We now have the "war on guns," "war on drugs," "war on crime," "war on racism" and "war on terror." There has been the creation of industries due to the misleading investigations. Saving the family, work, friends, belonging… is more important than stopping the drugs, terrorists, video games and the Alt-Right. The Ku Klux Klan for example, today has only 3,000 members nationwide. It is one of the oldest racist groups in America, yet it is losing popularity. I would still list them as a terrorist organization; however, dedicating programs to fighting them is not necessary. In 2002, 46% of court cases that were not related to terror were labeled as such anyway. Harsh sen-tences are being assigned everyday and this leads people to end up in prison while the public believes crime must be high. 65 million Americans have a criminal record even if it is a traffic violation; bankruptcy or something as mediocre as copying a DVD movie which would also result in a fine of $200,000. The violators are being registered as criminals.

Moreover, I can say with confidence that we do not have a gun problem in this country in the sense that the media tries to push. ISIS will not take over America. Crime is not high. Mentally

ill people are not on the loose and out to get us. Many of the terrorists who used guns did not have them registered under their own
name. For example, the Connecticut school terrorist used his
mother's gun to shoot 27 students, teachers and his own mother to
death. Therefore, we do not need more background checks. Even
those who call for gun control rarely push for a complete ban on a
particular gun. They believe we need more guns in schools to get
guns out of schools. It is disturbing to hear some of their so-called
solutions to terrorism and shootings. Some have even said teachers
need to be armed. What a scary scene it would be to have the terrorist shooting from one end of the classroom while the teacher
shoots from the other end. Activists do not call for reinstating the
1994 ban on assault rifles, which was able to reduce mass shootings for ten years. Their main call has been for more spying on
Americans and background checks; not the reduction of guns in
this country, which precisely proves the mental health industry.
Many of the advocates for the so-called "Black Lives Matter"
movement do not call for defunding police departments or reform-
ing the criminal justice system. They do not question the globalist
agenda. They demand attacks on right-wing groups and Neo-Nazis
that have no affiliation with the police, which precisely proves the
human rights industry.

Below is a key to help translate what each "war on…" means
and how we can be more careful when the next budget is being
passed:

"war on terror" = war industry
"war on drugs" = illegal drug industry
"war on racism" = human rights industry
"war on crime" = security industry/prison industry
"war on guns" = mental health industry

Every time there was a tragic event we chose to pull down the flag instead of sponsor connections. We chose to fight the substitutes instead of saving the things that make us feel we are part of something and prevent suicide, addiction, terrorism… through policies that are in fact less costly than the "war ons." "Walk to End Alzheimer's," "End Suicide" and "Mental Health Awareness Month" should be replaced with "Save our Families," "One Person, One Job" and "Compassion Counts." These titles sound like they tackle the causes of alienation such as unemployment and failing families; not the solutions to alienation like drugs and suicide. In his TED talk, Hari brought up how Portugal has removed the ban on most drugs. He says even though cocaine, marijuana, meth and other substitutes for connections are okay to have in Portugal it is rare that anyone chooses to purchase them. No one feels the need to use drugs even though they are freely available because the Portuguese government is heavily funding the family; creating jobs; connecting communities; and sponsoring traditions. Portugal does not have a "war on drugs." Instead it is spending 10.5% of its G.D.P. on education; has a 1.9% poverty rate; has a crime rate of 0.7; and has a smoking rate of 22.7. It has chosen to remove the barrier between humans and connections instead of placing a barrier between humans and substitutes. The Portuguese feel a sense of purpose and belonging. They are happy and do not feel alienated. They have many friends. Their cage is filled with all sorts of colorful things, meaning that there is basically no room left for drugs. In America, in order to make the "war ons" industries relevant we choose to call these actions socialism. We choose to ignore the statistics. We can never legalize drugs in this country because we have defunded the family. We have replaced humans and employed machines. Legalizing drugs would be a like a pandemic killing half of our population. Below is a graph showing the countries with the most and least spending on video games -- another popular substitute for genuine human connections:

21

## Countries' Spending on Video Games

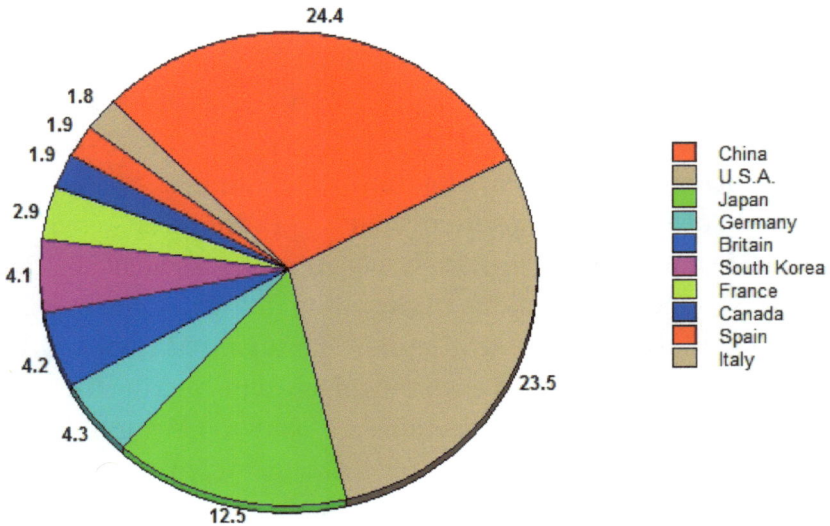

24.4

1.8
1.9
1.9
2.9
4.1
4.2
4.3
12.5
23.5

China
U.S.A.
Japan
Germany
Britain
South Korea
France
Canada
Spain
Italy

*Revenue earned through sales in billions of dollars

As we can see, Portugal does not even make it onto the list. The top ten countries that have the highest usage of video games are the countries that have least invested in connections such as families and work. All of these countries are also from the Global North, meaning they have the best economies, many freedoms, and conduct elections. Yet, these do not seem to satisfy the populations who feel without purpose and belonging. China can be qualified as an outlier since many freedoms are still banned in this country; however, economically China can be categorized with the Global North. All of these countries have been committed to the "war ons" and have spent heavily on fighting the substitutes instead of funding connections. There are over 1,271 agencies dedicated to fighting terror in America which are not actually listed under the same department. For example, the Bureau of Alcohol, Tobacco, Firearms and Explosives is not listed under the Department of Homeland Security; it is managed by the Department of Justice. Yet, the Department of

Homeland Security also has a similar agency with the same mission called the Federal Emergency Management Agency. In comparison, no other department but the Department of Health and Human Services has the duty to protect families and promote their well-being.

I have designated the Departments of Interior, Labor, Transportation and the Administration for Children & Families as agencies supporting connections and the Department of Defense and the Bureau of Alcohol, Tobacco and Firearms as agencies fighting substitutes. There are of course many more agencies that deal with both categories. However, finding even these statistics was very tough. The Department of Defense has a budget of $686 billion while the Department of Interior gets to have $11 billion. Where we put our money really shows what we see as real issues. The Department of Interior deals with land preservation and natural habitats. I will assume it as an agency meant for cultural heritage and museums as well; something similar to UNESCO. As I mentioned, culture is being defunded. Nature can be part of our culture too especially when there is Native American heritage involved. Yet, we do not see saving culture as a priority. It seems more important to fund the Department of Defense and "fight terror" in order to keep young men from finding connection with them. The Department of Labor has a budget of $9.4 billion while FEMA gets to have $13.9 billion.

In the case of my Canada voyage what substitute had the white population been busy with when they were not at C.N. Tower or Niagara Falls? From this I think the essential question we need to ask one another is: what's in your cage?

# PRIVATIZING HELP

I was fresh out of college when I decided to enter the world of volunteering and philanthropy. I guess it was mostly due to the fact that I still did not have a career but the experience is worth just as much as a full-time job. I looked into my local social services department and came across the food bank; an entirely government funded organization. On my first day the thing that most caught my attention was the donations of pet food. I thought it thoughtful that an organization committed to helping humans in poverty also has a heart for their dogs and cats. The next thing that caught my eye was the bonding between the volunteers. The way they communicated was as if they were longtime friends and everyone knew each other's name. After that I came across a section called the "free table." Here were all the non-food items and random stuff that usually the food bank does not receive. Some items were: calendars, holiday decorations, clothing, socks, school supplies and even electronics such as printers. Next I saw the fresh vegetables sitting on the back counter. They were provided by a local farmer who struggles with competition from abroad. One of the volunteers was the main promoter of him bringing in locally grown peppers, cabbage, tomatoes and potatoes. She coordinated the whole process of transferring them from the farm to the food bank. Above that counter were shelves stocking women's products and elderly pads. They were available in different brands, sizes and forms. Although we were sometimes low on women's products the pads for the elderly had much variety. After getting to know everyone I was overwhelmed by the large shipments of donations from department stores such as Big Lots, Aldi, Big Y and Stop & Shop. There were carts and carts full of meat and some dry products like candy or cereal. We had to weigh them before sending them to the freezer. The culinary school in town would sometimes donate their students' meals and dishes to the food bank. Even though the students were in training their meals still looked good and would immediately catch the attention of clients. There was macaroni and cheese, salads, pasta with chicken and of course hamburgers.

During the Christmas season the food bank has the Santa Fund. This is an opportunity for parents to select gifts for their children and have them ready for Christmas. The volunteers prepare a room with various new toys, clothing, books and music. The parents come in and choose whatever they see fit for their child depending on age and gender. Another program during this time is Sibling Shopping. On this day Santa Claus is also present at the food bank and takes pictures with the children.

That experience left me proud of what the government can do if given a chance. I learned much while I was over there. We throw out food when its expiration date has come but at the food bank there was a chart signaling all the types of foods that can still be used after the due date. The dates are more for the attention of supermarkets and vendors so that they sell the products quickly. Milk can still be drunk even after a few days past the date. Dry products even go as far as a year. I used that in my life and now I waste less food. I personally do not know of any private institution that offers the same products and services as the food bank as far as hunger goes. I have volunteered at numerous private and public organizations and each definitely has its own pluses and minuses. I teach English to immigrants twice per week at a private educational institute. There are many volunteers there similar to the food bank and they are all doing great work not only promoting the use and learning of the English language but also guiding immigrants in a new country and introducing them to the best schools for their children; finding jobs; getting their college degrees evaluated; and helping them obtain various documents such as library cards and marriage certificates. There are also citizenship and General Education Degree courses available. I believe this is the definition of changing people's lives. Next to this, however, I also noticed some flaws. The book the institute had given us to work with did not focus on dialogue which is the most important thing an immigrant should be able to do. The executive director always wanted to advertise the book in order to get funding and help from corporate donors. Private organizations are always asking for money and this sometimes interferes with their mission because they must always advertise the companies that helped them. They throw galas and parties which always attract rich investors. Although not all the students were new to America, the institute assumed my student could drive without permanent residency. They expected her to attend all the picnics and gatherings. However, my student always took the bus to class and being on a fiancé visa she still was not able to obtain her driver's license. Whenever the institute published newsletters or mail to students it was always in Spanish next to the English even though students came from a wide range of countries such as Albania, China, Bangladesh and Brazil. The most annoying thing at the food bank was the fact that sometimes there would be miscommunication between volunteers helping clients and volunteers in the storage room. When clients enter the food bank they are greeted by someone at the front desk and immediately checked in. They are able to enter and walk in the aisles (accompanied by a volunteer) as if they are walking in the supermarket. Some even carry carts or baskets to put their items in and take to their cars. The scene is truly impressive.

According to the Department of State, there exist 1.5 million private organizations in America working in areas such as the disabled and women's rights to health and the environment. Their official website mentions a lot about the freedoms and liberties of Non-Profit Organizations and one of them is tax exemption. N.G.O.s are not required to pay any amount of their income or donations to the government as tax money and therefore, are allowed to use all of their funds toward their missions and their employees. N.G.O.s also gain freedom of expression. The government is not allowed to meddle in their political views unless it has to do with money laundering, sponsoring terror or campaign financing. The next major plus for private organizations in America is being able to accept foreign money. There are no restrictions on who donates that money or for what reason. It could even be a foreign government that has been a threat to U.S. interests.

You probably receive a plethora of mail from N.G.O.s as I do ranging from international ones like Care to national ones like St. Jude with various missions and tasks. I have been generous to some of these but what I personally get disturbed by is their political correctness in their reporting. In a February 2020 letter from United Nation's International Children's Emergency Fund the organization was asking for help regarding the start of the new year and that I can "multiply the impact of my support five times" before April. Some of the areas in which they mentioned they were sponsoring were "children facing conflict, disease, malnutrition and limited access to safe water and sanitation." The next issue they touched was the Rohingya who fled Myanmar due to the genocide. But this was not what the letter stated. Their exact phrase was about a young boy who had escaped due to "violence" in the country and was seeking help in Bangladesh. Although this does not affect their efforts for humanity and the people they are supporting it did sound confusing to me as a donor who has been following the genocide in Myanmar. "Violence" could mean many things ranging from war to terrorism to riots to genocide. Why did they go for the general term?

Before that letter I had received an even more disappointing one from Care. After eight years of the presence of ISIS and other

28

terrorist groups Care was still referring to the situation as "a nearly decade-long civil war in Syria." A page and a half long, the letter did not contain a single phrase related to terror and terrorists. Not only was this politically correct, it was also not factual. According to Merriam-Webster civil war refers to "a war between opposing groups of citizens of the same country." ISIS is comprised of foreign nationals who have traveled to Syria from countries like Britain, Sweden, France and even the United States. Very few are actually Syrian.

Again, this does not affect the missions of Care, UNICEF or any other humanitarian N.G.O. out there. They are the ones on the scene and in the frontlines of many of the most horrific events the world has experienced. They have accomplished a lot with their donations. For instance, one N.G.O. I have been very pleased with has been Help Me See and its affiliate Help Me Smile. Help Me See does not hand out money; it hands out knowledge. It has been using donations to teach Manual Small Incision Cataract Surgery to eye surgeons and doctors in the developing world. Cataract removal seems like such an easy task, but many doctors in India, Bangladesh and Mexico do not know how to treat it. Help Me See also sends me letters and photos in the mail and so far I think they have been the least biased. But for what reason are the C.E.O.s and employees of these private institutions refraining from accuracy and truth? Even if it is to keep away from partisanship, is it not still indifferent and ignorant?

Private organizations have also shown bias in areas related to culture, health, housing and youth. When word came out that the two famous statues in Afghanistan known as the Buddhas of Bamian had been demolished by the Taliban UNESCO did nothing to protect it nor did it condemn it. It failed to show non-alliance with President Bush's war. Another instance where UNESCO backed away from its obligations was when ISIS had taken over the city of Palmyra in Syria. The Greco-Roman architecture had fallen into terrorist hands twice yet it was only the Syrian government that tried to protect it. Palmyra had been registered as a World Heritage Site; meaning UNESCO should have protected it regardless of what was happening in Syria. Much of it has also been destroyed by graffiti or looted and taken abroad. As mentioned, terrorists are not just trained to kill. Their mission is to also destroy the culture of the effected country.

The United Nations' Blue Helmets have bases all around the globe. They are basically the military branch of the U.N. and are made up of soldiers who serve their native countries' armies. Their task is to "keep the peace." That means they do not interfere for or against any government. They do not fight enemies. They do not prevent attacks. This is definitely unbiased behavior; however, it is not the kind the world needs. The Peacekeepers' official website lays out some of the main duties of the Blue Helmets: protect civilians, prevent conflicts, build rule of law and security institutions, promote human rights, empower women, and deliver field support. None of these efforts although worthwhile and surely needed match any of the world's current crises. For example, Blue Helmets are not required to fight terrorism. Terrorism is a global issue, yet no international organization is tasked with fighting it. The result has been the creation of an alliance of countries entering into the affected country and breaking rules of sovereignty. I contacted UNICEF on a different matter but somehow came across the issue of fighting terror. I asked why the U.N. in general refrains from fighting terror. The spokesperson on the phone said with sheer assertion that it is not the U.N.'s job to fight terror and that there are countries such as Russia who have picked up that task and are fighting terror today. If Peacekeepers are not tasked with fighting some the world's most common problems then why do we pretend to have them? Take a look at Palestine. Peacekeepers are supposed to calm down borders and prevent neighboring countries from breaking out, yet Israeli forces constantly cross over Palestinian territory and expand their border. Palestinians on the other hand come near the border and throw homemade devices. Palestine is one of the major areas where Blue Helmets have a presence but there seems to be more violence in the region when they are around.

Under principles of peacekeeping the U.N. outlines some very shocking points about the Blue Helmets. They are not allowed to use force under any circumstances unless they are under a direct threat or have approval by the Security Council. They say "... peacekeepers are not a substitute for political engagement to tackle root causes of conflict and violence." This highly restricted order disables the Blue Helmets from performing some of the most needed tasks the world requires such as fighting terror. It makes them look more like guards rather than a true global military force that protects everyone. It is no wonder why we have the segregation of security through institutions such as NATO. Poor and developing countries are supposed to depend on the Peacekeepers while rich and developed countries gain entrance into NATO, an organization that is more funded, more active and does not need approval from anyone to act. Their safety and security is guaranteed while the rest of the world waits for the Security Council, whose permanent members are all part of NATO; except for China and Russia.

In his book *The Great Convergence*, Kishore Mahbubani talks about the benefits globalization has had for the Global South. Published in 2013 I would say his book is a little late for the party we threw in the 1990s when globalization started its course. In this book he also talks about the flaws, struggles and failures of global organizations -- and he points out that their numbers are growing more than ever. New agencies are created every day for the same topics and issues rather than new topics or ones that have never received any attention at all like factory workers in China. Many have been unfaithful and robbed donor money through various fees and charges. Mahbubani says N.G.O.s or government agencies like USAID should never distribute free money in the name of foreign aid. Foreign aid is a form of bribery and this is always proven through political events. The countries we give aid to are always the ones supporting our policies (good or bad). They always buy our weapons and are the nations we can most easily influence. For instance, when Trump was chastised for cutting aid to Ukraine he claimed that President Zelenski was doing a political favor for Joe Biden. Everyone ignored what had been going on between Biden and Ukraine and all of the attention was directed toward how inhumane and cruel Trump was to cut aid to a former communist country being colonized by Russia. Similarly, the top countries that line up to buy our weapons are Pakistan, India, Israel and Saudi Arabia. These countries also receive large amounts of aid and always align themselves with our policies. Mahbubani supports my proclamation on the value of some organizations compared to others by stating that the institutions that deal with money, for example, are always led by a Western leader while institutions that are less favorable are always led by an Asian, African or Latin leader. The Secretary General of NATO is the Norwegian Jens Stoltenberg while the U.N. Secretary General is the Portuguese Antonio Guterres, the first time in six decades a European has held the position. Location has also shown to prove bias. Almost all of the world's global institutions today are headquartered in either New York, Washington, The Hague, or Brussels. None of them are located outside of Europe or North America. Take a look at the International Criminal Court. The United States is always in denial and in opposition to what the I.C.C. stands for and rules. It has constantly called for the prosecution and investigation of various American military officials and generals and called their cruel, degrading and inhumane actions in Afghanistan and Iraq as criminal. As always, we bring up the issue of national security to prevent truth from taking its course.

There are methods to reform these N.G.O.s and make them more responsive to people's complaints and questions even if their C.E.O.s and leaders are not chosen by citizens. As I mentioned, their overall intentions are good and they definitely care for the well-being of all people regardless of their country's financial status. However, the bias has to be removed and there needs to be more cooperation, incorporation and leadership of all countries in order to make these global institutions truly global. In the meantime we could also give more credit to what the government can do regarding help and assistance. We could look into our local public institutions more closely and see what they are doing with our tax money. We could volunteer and support the government. Taxes work the same way as donations do. They are meant to support public activities and the common good. Sometimes I get phone calls by N.G.O.s demanding I pay $15 for a good cause. It makes me feel I have to pay my taxes or that I am behind on a loan. It seems more annoying than an act of kindness. If we oppose taxation, then how come we willfully and proudly donate to private organizations that are committed to the same projects and programs our government is responsible for?

# OUR FAITH

America is a land with the most religious freedom anyone could have. However, I don't mean freedom of religion and the possibility of each citizen being able to worship whatever god he or she desires. I am referring to freedom from religion. Our schools do not require religious studies. The government does not require us to affiliate with a particular faith. We are not frowned upon for ignoring Easter or Sunday church. Our employers are not allowed to ask us if we believe in God let alone what religion we follow.

This is perhaps worth celebrating. However, what is it exactly that we do have faith in? If we are not fasting during Ramadan; or not celebrating bar mitzvahs; or ignoring Good Friday does it translate as us not having any faith at all?

A Pew Research study from 2010 reveals that it is true newer generations tend to be less and less able to identify with a particular religion. They are more open toward gay rights and more accepting of differing faiths such as Islam. But that does not translate as them being atheist or "non-believers" as a general term. Most youth today say they do believe in heaven and hell. Most think God exists. They help the poor. However, when it came to the choices on the survey they were hesitant to circle Protestant or Catholic.

I would say young people today are definitely spiritual. They look for meaning and something tranquil to relieve them of the stresses of city life, work and modernity. They may not be able to name what they believe in yet they are faithful and have set certain criteria for what they do and how they do it. It may not be the same criteria as their friends; however, their friends too have set criteria.

My recommendation is for us to construct spiritual courses throughout our universities. These could be free electives open to any student in whatever major or area of study. They need not be focused on any specific religion but rather they could be focused on health. I believe this helps young people be more open about religion and express their thoughts and views in an academic setting where professionals are present and no one gets criticized for what they think or identify with. They need not even be labeled as Catholic Studies or Jewish Studies. They can simply be coded as Spirituality classes so that students do not feel as if they have to decide if they are Catholic or Protestant.

Web M.D. reviewed a study in which it found that people who go to church, synagogue or the mosque are more likely to live longer. They are less prone to depression and anxiety and are better able to handle major events in their lives such as the loss of a loved one or poverty. They are less likely to feel lost and without hope. It does not call for people to go to church more often and it does not identify a particular religion. The study also suggests that one reason is because when people go to a place of worship they are exposed to other people and are provided an opportunity to socialize. They can make friends and limit isolating themselves in the home. Spirituality is related to health and how we feel about ourselves. It is more than just performing a set of practices; it helps us step out of just our own environment.

India is probably the most religiously diverse country in the world. They have large populations of Hindus, Muslims, Sikhs, Buddhists, Jains and Christians. There exist a lot of challenges with such varying faiths residing door to door, such as the constant violence against Muslims; however, what is remarkable in my view about faith in India is that every person believes in something bigger than they are and looks for guidance. Very few can proclaim they do not believe in any faith at all and do not think spirituality is important. This is perhaps a badge of honor for the country to wear given the studies we looked at by Web M.D.

The Organization for Economic Cooperation and Development ranked member countries in 2005 with the highest and lowest rates of suicide. Among those with the highest suicide rates are some of the most secular countries in the world such as South Korea, Japan, France, the United States, Canada and Britain. South Korea is number one on the list while France makes it to the top five. Although America does not even reach top ten it still has a rate of 10.1 per 100,000 people. I believe there is room for concern here and that we should put more effort into saving our own people from something as sad as suicide. These are the world's most advanced countries. There is no lack of water, democracy, or access to education. Women's rights are respected and citizens directly vote for their leaders. Why would people make such heartbreaking decisions? Maybe the better question is, why don't we see this as a threat to national security?

The WHO conducted a more recent study on suicide which included all the nations of the globe. Even among those countries I found that the ones with the highest rates also happen to be the countries with the most secularization. The former Communist countries which used to have religion prohibited lead the way, with Russia ranking number one in the world at a rate of 48.3 per 100,000 people. Next is the United States, South Korea, Japan and Finland ranking in the 20's range. Australia and Canada come in third ranking above 15. The graphs below compare the suicide rates of secular and non-secular countries:

# Secular & Non-Secular Countries Suicide Rate

## Secular & Non-Secular Countries

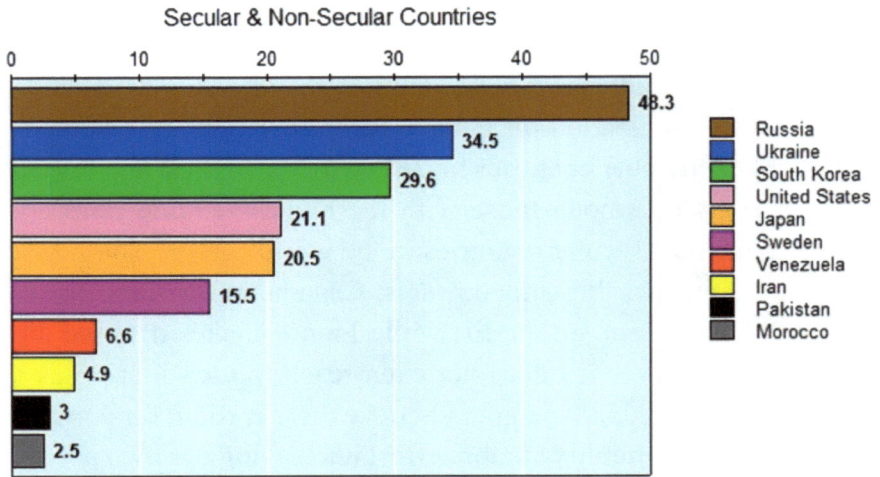

| |  |
|---|---|
| Russia | 48.3 |
| Ukraine | 34.5 |
| South Korea | 29.6 |
| United States | 21.1 |
| Japan | 20.5 |
| Sweden | 15.5 |
| Venezuela | 6.6 |
| Iran | 4.9 |
| Pakistan | 3 |
| Morocco | 2.5 |

Suicide Rate

*Data is for male citizens

# Secular & Non-Secular Countries Suicide Rate

## Secular & Non-Secular Countries

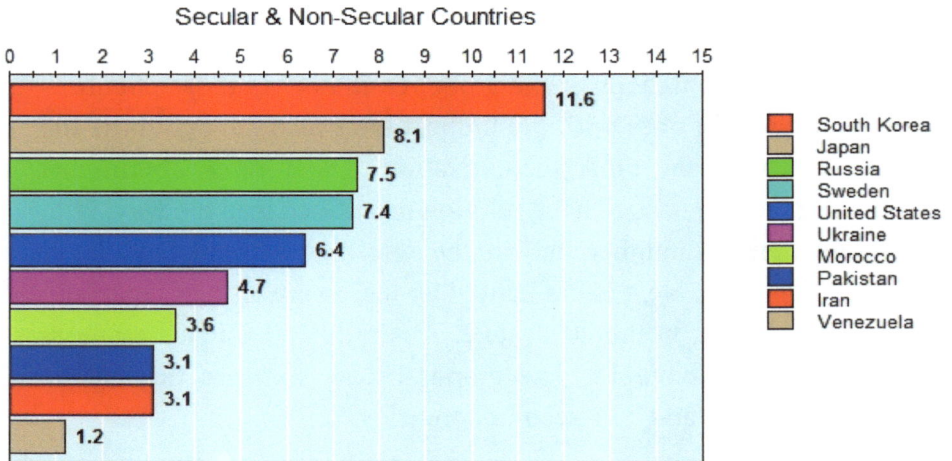

| |  |
|---|---|
| South Korea | 11.6 |
| Japan | 8.1 |
| Russia | 7.5 |
| Sweden | 7.4 |
| United States | 6.4 |
| Ukraine | 4.7 |
| Morocco | 3.6 |
| Pakistan | 3.1 |
| Iran | 3.1 |
| Venezuela | 1.2 |

Suicide Rate

*Data is for female citizens

Again, this is not to suggest that people in secular countries should claim more religiosity and go to church more often or limit freedom from religion. But the statistics do show that countries we have come to traditionally know as more strict in their religious beliefs like Pakistan are in fact at a lower risk of suicide than secular countries like South Korea. Women are generally less likely to commit suicide than men, yet even their numbers are higher in secular countries than women living in non-secular countries.

In America, there has always been the fear that religion might take over similar to the European churches and their rule throughout history. However, if we believe that we have established democracy and the existence of various rights we should not be afraid of the rise of religion. Most of the non-secular countries today are also developing countries. That means democracy has not fully been achieved and there exist many economic, political and social struggles. America is not a developing nation. There is no need for us to fear losing secularism. Therefore, we can be more spiritual (not religious) and live in a democratic society at the same time.

# OUR EDUCATION

When I graduated from high school I was on my way to the world of politics and government at Western Connecticut State University. I was excited and thought I am prepared now for not just higher education but also the world of adulthood and independence. It was a proud feeling. Passing all those diverse subjects from physics to physical education is a requirement and necessary for your background as a student. Although many of those classes were essential to my life, I think there were some life skills that many critics would agree were lacking in my education.

For example, the only cooking experience I ever had was in 8th grade. A half credit course focused on the essentials of the kitchen and basic cooking methods. My class of under ten students learned how to bake cookies and pizza. We cleaned the kitchen. We washed the dishes and put back the ingredients. It was fun and opened our world to a different environment. The most useful tip I still remember to do is to move the lid toward the stove before lifting it from the pot so that the heat doesn't hurt my face. The other half credit went towards sewing and knitting. I was exposed to working with the sewing machine and the various knitting methods. We were working on sewing pillows and stuffing them with cotton.

After that I was never again exposed to culinary skills and the kitchen nor the sewing machine. What is ironic is that I am present in my kitchen every day preparing either breakfast or a small snack for myself. I wash the dishes when my mom is busy and I chop vegetables from the supermarket. Every time I let her down. I feel disappointed for not being educated on the most common activities we do as humans on a daily basis. Sure, I will need Pi in my life but I also need to eat pie! Would it be a loss to cut back on one of our current subjects in school in order to fund something as common as cooking?

Many children and their parents ask "when am I ever going to need the table of contents?" or "why should I take a second language when all the world speaks English?" It is obvious that these courses are necessary and there is no way of getting out of them. They are needed for a college application but are they used just as often in real life? In his book "Excellent Sheep" William Deresiewicz goes over the stresses students endure in order to get accepted at highly acclaimed colleges such as Harvard and Yale. They take A.P. classes, sports, play in the band AND sing in the chorus in order to appeal to counselors and admissions departments. He says this creates a sense of loss and pointlessness. Students are, for instance, playing in the band not because they necessarily like music but because they are trying to grab attention and get accepted. They become lawyers not to, for example, defend workers' rights or as a sense of passion, but to attain money, status and power. Money does not act the same way as passion and therefore, we have many Wall Street pollutants who are Harvard, Princeton and Yale graduates. Real life evil geniuses. Deresiewicz says this is because students do not know how to use their knowledge so they decide to just focus on making the cash.

Those who don't go to college probably lose the most. They not only lack the essential life skills such as cooking, sewing and cleaning they also cannot compete in the workforce. In a globalized world a college education is a must. This I am not resisting. However, what I am encouraging is for our 12 years of free education to be more connected to our real lives and our real experiences. What good is a bachelor's in political science if you do not have good communications skills, lack confidence and cannot speak in public? I would even recommend bringing driver's education into the school system as one of the essential life skills courses. Isn't driving and travel one of the top activities humans do on a daily basis? If my dad was never into gardening and flowers I probably never would have learned about the different plants and trees that exist; not even in my science classes. Gardening is fun and an activity that is used in real life. However, I was never exposed to it in school. My dad covers our entire house with beautiful sunflowers and petunias. He collects the seeds of tomatoes and pumpkins during the fall so that he can plant them again next year. One year we were able to harvest three pumpkins just in time for Halloween. Other times we are constantly harvesting zucchini, peppers and tomatoes. Whatever I know about gardening is because of him and helping him out all summer. Our education needs to be more hands on and outside of the classroom setting. This is worth the sacrifice.

High school is not the only incomplete education experience we have. My four years of education in politics at W.C.S.U. also had flaws. I was never trained for any profession. 121 credits went toward classroom instruction and theory. I never had hands on, in action, experience, and that void has produced its own consequences. I have been unemployed for three years and have been learning work through social organizations and volunteer work that no employer is ever going to consider as work experience. I have never been paid for anything and feel disappointed in myself because I lack skills. You might say well, why didn't you apply for internships and temporary positions offered to students? I actually did find one at my state capital yet the transportation was my main problem. Next to that I also had to find references and recommendations from my professors.

I believe we need to revise our method of educating people. The classroom system is obsolete and limits the world of students. Students need to get exposed; they need to meet different people;

visually learn something instead of just picturing it in their minds. That is why I am a big fan of career approached education. Fields like medicine and the military are definitely hands on and more active than history or politics. Students spend more time training and less time on a computer or writing in their notebooks. Once they graduate they possess so many valuable skills that can be used in not just the medical field or the army but also in communications, business, law and coaching. Think about athletes. Do they ever spend time in a classroom environment? Do they ever stare at a board? They are constantly moving their bodies and learning through hands on experience. Their skills can be used in not just the stadium or arena but also in social work, culinary, education and medicine. My brother is a bodybuilder. He has been training since he entered high school and has been steadily improving since then. He follows all the popular bodybuilders such as Phil Heath, Kai Greene and Beytollah Abbaspour. In watching their training videos he has not only become a bodybuilder but also a chef! Eating is a huge part of bodybuilding and if you do not know how to cook then you should probably leave the sport. My brother can chop vegetables, roast chicken, boil rice and fry potatoes. This is aside from his daily fruit shakes and vitamin oriented meals. He did not intend to become a good cook but through a totally different field he used his skills in bodybuilding and introduced them to cooking.

In comparison, whenever I talk about Trump to my family or how the elites are promoting a coup against him they get annoyed and ignore me. My dad sometimes starts a conversation with me but in general I feel like I annoy them more than enlighten them. This reminds me of how many employers are going to even ask me about any of the stuff I learned in university or high school. Who will ask me about the flaws in our criminal justice system? Who will require me to know about the Bill of Rights? In comparison, my brother's skills in bodybuilding will always be asked of him even in his current job at a pharmaceutical company.

## COLD WAR II A GUIDE TO WHAT WE CAN DO; NOT A EULOGY

Look at Arnold Schwarzenegger. He was a professional bodybuilder yet somehow entered the world of politics and art. What does bodybuilding have to do with being a good politician? Maybe the sense of confidence and self-esteem that is required for body-building helped him become such a popular governor. Maybe his muscular form and appearance seemed attractive enough for movies like "The Terminator" and "Conan the Destroyer." My point is that when we think more about how we are going to use our knowledge in something we end up becoming more goal oriented and have a clear future for ourselves. Our studies in geography, math, history, politics and literature are not providing enough activity and hands on experience. When we take these classes we are mostly in the classroom setting without any clear decision about how we are going to put what we learned into use. We do not get trained in archeology and travel numerous times to Egypt to solely uncover the history of the country piece by piece. We do not visit a building under con-struction in order to find out how numbers are really used by an en-gineer. These activities are not only training but also fun experiences and unforgettable. I may have forgotten what I learned in geometry, but I will always remember visiting that engineer and imitating his acts at the workplace. Many universities and even high schools offer travel abroad programs, visits to museums, internships and invite guest speakers. These are truly exciting and heavily sponsored ex-amples of hands on learning. However, how many students can af-ford to, for example, go to Germany? How many students are going to have the GPA requirements to work next to a real Congressman? My high school asked for over $2,000 from students in the German class in order to take them to Germany and provide them with the opportunity to actually use the German language with native speak-ers instead of the classroom. Of course not everyone could afford to go but those who were better off still remember that trip and in fact still remember the German language.

Life skills are all about hands on experience. When I was taking cooking and sewing classes in 8th grade I never took notes or stared at a board. I was always working on the machine or turning on the stove. When I applied for my driver's license, I was in a car most of the time and spent some lessons in the classroom. This is not a call to abandon the classroom but we can revise and update our teaching methods and system in order to reflect what society will be asking from us in the future as adults. Every job you apply for either in the skilled labor force or education based labor force you will be asked to possess good communications skills, high confidence, professionalism and assertiveness. These are what will be asked of us in the first place. Employers want to know how we can do things with our hands. Second comes our knowledge of the particular subject.

When I graduated I thought knowledge and education were enough to enter the workforce. I thought all I needed was a degree and that that would be all that employers would need from me. I totally missed training and work experience, so here I am wandering around looking for ways to learn professionalism and skills. Our education needs to reflect what society will be needing and the hiring requirements various jobs possess. We cannot be teaching things to our students that no one will ever ask of them. When I go to the post office to mail a package the worker always says there is something wrong with the packaging or how I wrote the address. She says I need to go back home and fix it. I have overpaid many times due to lack of knowledge in shipping. None of my teachers ever taught me how to send a package or mail. My teachers never even taught me PowerPoint, Excel, Word or even social media. When I was revising my resume at W.C.S.U. my counselor said to write these down as skills! Until the 2011-2012 school year cellphones were banned in school. After that the school introduced B.Y.O.D. which means Bring Your Own Device. This was when school officials realized that social media and the internet are part of what employers will be asking of students in the future; therefore, putting a ban on their use does not help students learn how to utilize these needed skills.

Indeed, social media is not just for fun anymore. Today, many companies are doing business on Facebook, Twitter and Instagram. Social media managers get paid to post things for the company. It's basically a career. In fact, after B.Y.O.D. our school created its own page on Twitter and used it to make various announcements to students and their parents. My teachers never taught me a lesson on Microsoft programs but rather tried to introduce them through the various projects and presentations we had to do for class. For example, in 10th grade we had to complete a PowerPoint presentation about various empires in South America. Our teacher never went through how to make the PowerPoint but rather we were supposed to learn it through the assignment with which we were tasked. Personally, I think the PowerPoint was more important than the lesson on empires. Which do you think I am asked about more often today?

Lack of jobs is not the only issue we have in this country. There is also a lack of experiences, training and skills. Even if there does exist a well-paying and decent job if I am not qualified then it is as if there are no jobs for me. Employers today have so many requirements and expectations that go beyond just getting an education. One has to be confident, assertive, a good communicator and be able to follow the rules. I am very mad at all the organizations I applied to who denied me. They did not say I was unqualified; this I learned myself. Most of them said the economic conditions did not allow them to add anyone. Others said that I was good but they do not need anyone at this time. No employer acts as a humanitarian. They don't care about making sure every young person has a job. They want to fulfill their requirements and do not even tell the candidate to work on their skills and maybe apply next year. They just turn people down as if they were the first organization the person looked to for a job and that there are plenty of other places this person can look into. Well, that is certainly not the case and there definitely are not too many options. (This applies to other things as well and we will venture through it in "Our Family".) I have been looking for years and you are not the first organization I have applied to. But you do not care how long I have been looking. You are not a charity. You are not looking to reduce the number of unemployed people. You are selfish and just want to pay the people who are worth it.

Let me say it openly; I am not a good rule follower. My problem has always been that I like to invent ways of doing things. It's hard for me to follow directions. I possess too much creativity. This is obvious in my volunteering at the food bank. Sure, I do everything that is asked of me; I don't do whatever I want or change the plan and I definitely get the job done, but I noticed in myself that I always want to place items the way I want. For example, we have a gluten free section and an organic section at the food bank. Anything that is labeled gluten free or organic by the company must be placed on those designated shelves. When I see organic bread I automatically put it on the organic shelf but then one of the volunteers told me not to and that it should be mixed in with all the other bread on the bread rack. I agreed but inside I thought isn't it organic? Isn't it easier for clients to find organic bread on the organic shelf than on the bread rack?

Sometimes I need to control myself. At home when I have nothing to do I start organizing my parents' and my brother's rooms. Most of the time they thank me but other times they feel that their privacy has been invaded and tell me to not touch their stuff. I really don't know how to control it but I guess that means I need to find a creator job. Something like entrepreneurialism or a personal business. Anyway, being able to do things is more important than what is in your brain. Following exactly what is asked of you assures reliability on the part of the employer. Skills are what get you in the position; education is what keeps you there.

Many young Americans today probably have one of the biggest fears in their lives: tuition debt. They have called for reducing at least some amount of what they owe or to just waive the whole payment all together. Many want their children to at least see the day when college is free like some European nations and that they do not have to make the choice between living without higher education or sinking in thousands of dollars' worth of school debt.

Their concerns are real and in fact being a student myself I can certainly relate to what my generation is talking about. I have not yet calculated what I owe but I still do not have a job so I would say my situation is probably the worst out there. However, I have another major concern. Through what method are we going to fund education if we cut student loans? Also, how is the government going to replace all the money it gave away in financial aid in the years prior to forgiving loans?

The Department of Education was last reported to contain a budget of $68 billion. The Department of Defense reported $686 billion. Those numbers are really not comparable and are in fact disappointing. They resemble what our priorities are and what areas we would rather sacrifice in order to fund those priorities. President Trump called for the total abolishment of the Department of Education. My question is what is plan B? Could the private sector really handle such a broad subject? Or are we going to relocate education in full to the states and have it solely be a part of state duties to create policies on education?

My recommendation is to go back to the drawing board. Go back to the first chapter titled "Our Money." As long as we are dedicating such large amounts toward the war industry, the prison industry and many other shameful industries, we cannot provide free college education to Americans. The math does not allow it. We must abandon those areas and focus on what we really care about. We must weigh the ups and the downs. Would universities really do better if tuition is removed under current conditions?

If you are concerned with paying back your loans my suggestion is, don't be. When we demand something we force the government to keep all programs and funds related to that thing. We show interest and concern. If we back away from funding education it would mean we do not care enough about it. It would mean demand for education is low and therefore, the government should not bother to put money towards it. That applies to not just education. We must demand government fund health care, the postal service, social security and transportation. For example, whenever I use eBay or sell my textbooks online I always try to click on the United States Postal Service. I rarely choose Federal Express or United Parcel Service. Even though I might think FedEx is faster or more reliable I still go with the post office because I want to force the government to fund the program. I want to show demand is high and that Americans still rely on the post office so that the government does not ever think about shutting down the service. So that it is forced to renovate mailboxes; hire more workers; sanitize its hallways; and modernize its system. When I was five years old I remember going to the post office with my dad. We lived in Florida at the time and I believe it was the Hollywood area USPS we used. The entire hallway was infested with roaches. They were jumping up and down in the corner of the halls right next to where people were waiting in line. I wanted to leave but I had no choice because we had to send our package. The same is true of our state programs. We have all had that same experience at our Department of Motor Vehicles. Angry employees, dirty hallways, long lines and much paperwork. Fortunately, there still has not been a private competitor for automobile services and licensing so the government is forced to keep the facilities running.

These are our basic rights. Free education is only good when it is not a sign of bankruptcy on the part of government. When the Soviet Union failed in the 1990s Russia was in debt. It was the worst and only decade for President Yeltsin. He was forced to privatize everything that used to be under the government's control. Now, I fear we are headed the same direction. We have a major debt in the trillions. We have started defunding some of the most precious programs and policies Americans have come to relate to and depend upon. Many immigrants come all the way to America to take advantage of our most prestigious universities. Those who are on visa cannot apply for financial aid and so are willing to pay out of their own pockets for a good education. It is sad that we choose to exclude ourselves from this life changing experience because we fear tuition.

# OUR "VICTIM" JUSTICE SYSTEM

All throughout high school and college I was reminded of the importance of elections and that elections are one sign that democracy exists in a country. In the state of Connecticut, students are required to take Civics classes twice throughout their educational experience. This is how much elections and voting are emphasized in this state. Elections are the most popular method citizens get to be active and participate in civic duties. It is basically the only time they get to express what they think and whether they agree with something or not. Other forms exist too such as protests or referendums but elections are more peaceful in comparison. After entering the criminal justice field, I zoomed in on the fact that Americans vote for the Executive branch; they vote for the Legislative branch, too, yet they do not vote for the Judicial branch. That is, we vote for the President; we vote for Congressmen but in most cases we do not vote for judges. These are men and women who make some of the most controversial and life-altering decisions imaginable with the many cases they deal with on a daily schedule. They basically make laws out of cases that could affect over 300 million citizens!

Americans have witnessed a lot in the criminal justice system. We have many parents behind bars. Many young men. Families have separated due to the prison industry. For example, is it legitimate for someone who has used drugs but not sold them to be sentenced to 10 years in prison while those who are part of the industry are left loose? In many countries, drug use is considered an illness and violators are taken to rehabilitation; not prison. What is even more disappointing is that status and rank has also influenced our system. Would a rich football player with a long and prestigious background from a very admired team be sentenced the same way for committing the same crime? Is it humane for a pregnant woman to be kept in the prison environment for 9 months until her child's birth?

When the Las Vegas terrorist committed the horrific attacks at the M.G.M. hotel, families and victims of the event were looking for answers and retribution. What is sad is that the only answer they got was more rants on gun control and that the shooter was mentally disturbed. TV news channels totally ignored accountability and responsibility and chose to focus on guns falling into the wrong hands. They pretended to blame the government for not doing more background checks and spying on American citizens in order to stop the allocation of various guns to troubled and mentally unstable people. The victims never got a true answer until three years later when M.G.M. decided to give away $800 million to families of those who were killed for no reason other than having fun at a concert. After that the victims were quiet. They did not want to look into the shooter's past and did not have an interest in suing M.G.M. If this is not bribery, what is? We will never know how involved the hotel was in the attack and the managers will never be held accountable for not being able to prevent such a terrifying event. Other giants who regularly get off the hook are Facebook, Twitter and Google. They know people use their websites to regularly post violence, shame and bullying yet refuse to do anything to limit user activity in the name of freedom of speech. Many families and victims have also filed cases against them but with no surprise they too were excused for their deeds.

In October 2008, the media was heavily covering the tragic murder of a two-year old girl named Caylee. Her mother Casey Anthony had been arrested for not just killing her own daughter but also different instances of theft, lying and fraud. The theft and the fraud were unrelated to the major case; however, they were affecting how Americans viewed Anthony as a person. Caylee had been missing for more than a month, yet her mother never showed any signs of concern nor did she call the police. I was in 8<sup>th</sup> grade and remember constant images of the child and mother being played back to back by TV news channels. In 2011, Anthony was determined not guilty by the courts yet the charges for the other crimes remained on her name. Even then I was sad about the authorities totally ignoring who killed Caylee. If it was not the mother then they should have continued investigating until they found the real murderer. After more than a decade Caylee's killer is still wandering around free. This brings up the issue of victims' rights. If it was proven that Anthony did not kill her own child then that is definitely a good outcome for her. Congratulations. Justice was served on her part but what about justice for Caylee? Authorities closed the case after that verdict. They did not focus on the victim; they focused on the suspect. This is another issue we have in the American criminal justice system. Suspects get full attention while victims especially if they are dead never get adequate recognition. My question is who killed Caylee? Isn't this a concern for the mother? Shouldn't she be more sympathetic than any of us? In America when someone is found innocent it is as if no crime occurred at all. In relation to the Anthony case, since Anthony is innocent therefore, Caylee was not killed, and it is as if she is still alive. This bizarre form of "reasoning" is very sad especially when there is someone such as a child who cannot stand up for herself. If Anthony did not kill her child, then, in the eyes of the law, it does not matter who did.

In 1985, Edward Garner was shot by police during a chase. He was suspected of a home burglary and had been on the run. As he was climbing a fence one of the officers shot Garner in the head. He died on the scene. The courts first rejected any claims that Garner was treated with harsh confrontation and excessive force by the police. Yet when Garner's father sued, the Supreme Court stepped in and reversed the verdict by saying the Fourth Amendment was violated, even though the amendment only concerns searches and seizures. It was furthered to include the prohibition of use of force by police unless the suspect is armed. Garner was granted justice but what have we witnessed years later? What have we been protesting since that case? If the Fourth Amendment protects against the inappropriate and illegal use of force by police then why did we witness so many back to back shootings and maltreatment of young boys, most of them African-American? Why haven't the judges and the Supreme Court called out these instances of injustice to not only end the cycle but make a stand for themselves and show the public that the Constitution is real and cannot be manipulated?

The study of criminal justice has proven that punishment does not prevent or deter crime. That is not just applicable to criminals. Whenever we hear of police beating someone to death or unjustifiably pulling a gun we immediately call for the firing of that officer. Firing, however, has not helped reduce police aggression against unarmed African-Americans. Violators need to be rehabilitated for lack of a better term. They need to undergo ethics classes and morality. "One bad apple" has surely become five bad apples and the theory has failed. Firing individuals does not refurbish the system because it has too much corruption and the existence of folkways. In America, only 1/3 of police have a bachelor's degree. This is when it is not required by officials at all to possess a college education. When individuals begin their process of entering the field of law enforcement and the criminal justice system they immediately start training. That is, they do not start with academics and are in fact not required to undergo academic evaluations. Future police enter the workforce without prior education and academic knowledge. This is quite shocking given the fact that globalization requires everyone to get an education yet the police seem to still abide by the norms and traditions of the department and long-time officers who become their mentors. They show them how it has always been and that all they should do is copy traditional beliefs and practices. In the training process they learn virtually nothing about ethics and respect for suspects. What they do learn is racial profiling; the idea that black people are poor so they could never own a luxury car; and that all terrorists are Muslim. Future police officers easily pick up these routine beliefs, internalize them, and consider this now engrained mindset as training for their new job. The academy is irrelevant to officials and the students, which leaves plenty of space for organizational culture to feed into the minds of new recruits.

The organizational culture still exists once those forceful officers are out, therefore leaving the likelihood of another illegal act by yet another police officer very high. It is an entire ideology we are fighting against, not a particular individual police officer. This ideology is based on dehumanization and degradation of particular groups like women, black men, Muslims, people of war torn countries, children, animals … which is also present in our military. In fact, many of the criminal acts committed by police are the same criminal acts committed by soldiers and generals in the various wars we are involved in around the world. When soldiers raid homes in Afghanistan or Iraq they steal objects and furniture belonging to the family. They hold unarmed women and children hostage and go through the same pat downs as police do in America. Sexual harassment and degradation of women is also present in the Army. A similar situation is witnessed with police who use prostitute services. Soldiers are taught to shoot young children who come their way because it is always certain that they carry a bomb. Officials who are supposed to be civil servants and serve their people have been taught to view certain groups as less than human – and they have been trained with our money, and we pay their salaries. This gives them the right (they believe) to treat for instance, African-Americans the way they do. If degradation is something that is taught and injected into the brains of future police, then it is not an issue related simply to a particular officer's personality. We cannot conclude that if he or she were to have taken just an extra course on the slave trade, women's suffrage or the Holocaust as a student in school then he or she would not have treated black suspects with cruelty and oppression.

The same is assumed of terror suspects. We like to pretend terror is imported. However, radicalization happens right here and is exported to Muslim and Arab countries. Facebook and Twitter are mostly banned in Muslim countries so how could their people ever even try to view terror propaganda and videos even if they wanted to do so? Fewer failing families exist in these countries. Tradition is still relevant. There is a sense of purpose unlike in the West. No one needs to join terrorist organizations in these countries. No one comes to America as a terrorist. By the same token, these police officers did not come into power as racist individuals. They became racist and absorbed the culture of cruelty once they got the job. Therefore, it is a view we are suffering from; not the police force. This view is present while the elites claim to sponsor human rights, defend women, call out racism, and promote the election of non-white people like Barack Obama. How could they dehumanize these groups while also defending their rights? This is called the human rights industry. Police, the courts, prisons and the military share a culture of oppression yet try to also fight it on the other end. The media covers every case of abuse of African-Americans while supporting their killers. This was evident when Chelsea Manning, the former Army soldier in Iraq decided to expose the culture of cruelty through the British website called Wikileaks. Manning was exposing the same abuses and crimes committed by American police officers against young black men, yet she was labeled as a spy by the media and unpatriotic and disloyal to her country. The courts did not defend her cause and sentenced her to 35 years in prison. This was in addition to the national security excuse we are always confronted with when demanding the government to be honest with us. The government quickly rolled out the Espionage Act to justify racism and cruelty against Iraqi civilians, especially since it was a faraway land and who was going to be there to film it with their cell phone anyway?

CNN was one of the first news channels to come out against the Muslim ban and call it racist. I personally view it as a form of soft power against countries we like to demonize because in the end there were other countries added to the list that were not Muslim like Venezuela and North Korea. If Cuba and Russia get added to the list I would not be surprised. However, CNN also promoted all the wars against Muslim countries we are involved in and totally censured the liberation of Aleppo in 2016. Syrians were dancing in the streets while Western media was mourning for the terrorists. Hypocrisy and the culture of oppression are not something that will go away by simply firing violators or calling out racism. It may sooth the families for a while but that is until the next young black man is killed.

The death penalty has been a matter of concern for Americans for years whenever it comes to criticizing the American judicial system. In fact, it is one of the many flaws they claim the system has next to the prison industry. They view it as a form of cruel and unusual punishment even for the most violent of criminals such as rapists and terrorists. The death penalty is controversial and many prisoners fear becoming faced with it the next time they appear in court. However, statistics show that this method of punishment is in fact very rarely considered by judges. In Connecticut, the last time a prisoner was sentenced to death was in 1975. Connecticut became a death penalty-free state in 2012 so that is almost a forty year difference. None of the Colorado or Orlando terrorists were sentenced to death either. They were assigned life in prison, (formal or informal which I will explain). My concern is life sentencing. Many who vote for the abolition of the death penalty rely on prison for life as the next best option. The result has been suicide and self-harm all throughout our prisons. Many for-life prisoners are depressed as a result of knowing they will forever be closed off from the world outside. In Texas alone, there was a 40% increase in the number of suicides in prison from 2008 to 2014. Life sentencing is one reason behind why we have so many people in prison. It is not the number of prisoners that causes the inconsistency but rather the number of years judges assign to criminals that helps the prison population to grow while the crime rate goes down.

One example is informal life sentencing; that involves sentences of ridiculous ranges like 50 years, 80 years and even 100 years. These are informal life sentences because it is obvious the prisoner would not live long enough to serve his or her entire term. They would die before they are able to step out of prison and live a normal life again. Even if they do theoretically make it out after 80 years, how long is a life of old age without retirement and a criminal background going to last? Isn't informal life sentencing a form of cruel and unusual punishment too?

I am not in favor of executions or euthanasia, but life sentencing is not very appealing and can in fact be just as hazardous to the criminal justice system. We need to think of better substitutes and replacements as next best options. Life sentencing is more of a threat right now than the death penalty. Judges are more likely to select life sentencing than the death penalty as forms of punishment. We have more people serving life sentences than being executed by authorities. According to Forbes magazine there were 34,000 people serving life sentences in 1984. By 2016 that number had increased five times and has not gone down since. We need to do everything we can to lower prison sentences and get people out as soon as possible.

Other instances of injustice are present in other areas too. Take a look at our voting system known as the Electoral College. For years, Americans have been criticizing the system and witnessing its undemocratic traits. The 2000 presidential election is all too famous to be ignored in this book. When Vice President Al Gore and Governor George Bush were stuck on their electoral votes they relied on Florida to predict the winner of the election. Votes were discarded due to mismanagement at the polling stations; recounting of votes was taking place without constitutional approval and weeks had passed since election day. When the Supreme Court finally came to a decision it was heavily divided with 4 judges favoring Gore and 5 judges favoring Bush. They basically excused themselves from deciding on the case and were able to show that more accurately when they passed down the case to the Florida courts to decide. Florida dismissed the case. Gore had won the people's vote yet the Supreme Court was unprepared for such a day when electoral votes would come in short. All the news stations and papers were focused on a single state that had to take the burden. Perhaps if President Bush had been more admirable nowadays we would not have criticized the Electoral College but what could explain the incompetency of the judges and their time management? Why hadn't the Supreme Court called out the partial recounting of votes and the 14th Amendment earlier? Why did they put pressure on Florida so that they refuse to take the case at all? The Electoral College is an issue on its own but in 2000 we also had to deal with the unpreparedness of the courts.

My way out of this embarrassing and hazardous route is for us to be able to elect our own judges at both the national and state level. Electing judges equals accountability. It means when laws are made directly out of the courtroom, Americans have the right to stand up and object if it hurts their family. Judges would represent the people similar to the President, Senators and members of the House of Representatives. They would be required to answer the public and make revisions to the system that has made noise even outside our borders. The whole world knows we have 25% of the global prison population. People with various backgrounds, innocent and guilty, poor and rich and white and black. This does not go well with our rants about democracy and the sanctions we impose on countries who violate human rights. They can rightfully use it against us in a very legitimate way and therefore, make the American criminal justice system a threat to national interests.

Of course, elections can only work if there is no sponsoring and financing involved. My aim is not for judges to be treated like career politicians or presidential rivals who each own multiple homes in gated communities. I do not wish to add to the bribing and influencing of courts. Judges need to stay true to their voters because in the end it is they who would seek reelection and want to represent the system again. States have different regulations on election campaigns and advertising. Elections are handled by the states even if national elections are about to be conducted such as for the presidency. They dictate what is legal and illegal for candidates to do in order to get the public's attention and make them eager to come to the polls. Many states prosecute or even jail candidates for doing illegal activity in their campaigns. This is of course separate from the fact that cheating and lying is also illegal and unethical.

In Connecticut, if one were to run for governor, mayor or any other government position they would be required to follow strict elections rules. Therefore, I would recommend the qualified candidate to appeal to the public in such a way that it would show his or her respect for the law. Candidates want to stand out, reach out to the most alienated in society and spend a lot for each of these goals. Therefore, it is wise to spread flyers, brochures and mailings to local schools, homes, businesses and public services. Such activity is not illegal in Connecticut. Many candidates have reached out to people through mail without ever asking for that resident's address or permission. That is because once we register to vote our personal information becomes available for the government.

I believe reaching out to the young is the most important step in our time today. Young people have become alienated and they are struggling. They have lost confidence in the system in general and can no longer fully align themselves with either of the major parties.

They have soaring education levels, high preschool and babysitter fees, low wage jobs and no form of government support that could lift them out of poverty. I would suggest to the running candidate to make youth his or her top priority when getting voters to the polls.

The second effective method would be giving speeches in public areas where the most people are present. They may be conducting their daily activities such as shopping but when confronted with a candidate at the mall for example, they may stop to hear his or her voice. This is a legal and most attractive method because voters are busy and have heavy schedules to abide by. Many people do not vote simply because they do not have enough background information on the candidate. A public speaking event is most reliable to get the word out while also adhering to state laws and regulations. This is not to say that the public area must be in full support of the candidate. Libraries, schools, malls and town halls only serve as places where people gather. It is not to show that these institutions back the candidate.

A third legal and ethical method to get voters out is to offer rides to the polling stations. Free merchandise and services has never been illegal under Connecticut law and many candidates have taken advantage of the opportunity. This is especially needed due to the fact that public buses do not make it a priority to drive passengers to the polls. Although it is a public event, public transportation does not fully support it. Therefore, free rides to the polls can be encouraging and hassle free in the eyes of voters.

Fourth, it is highly valuable in election practices for candidates to avoid siding with the next best candidate if they are not to win the election. Although candidates come from the same parties, the notion of party voting is disappearing in America. Americans are identifying less and less with party ideology and more with the issues. They are attracted to the candidate who talks about preserving the environment, saving tax money for infrastructure repair, fixing failing families... Party voting is not associated with newer generations of voters. In fact, it is not even required by state law for candidates to have in mind the next best choice if they are not to win. Therefore, I would advise my candidate to campaign based on issues and not on party ideology.

Polling and surveying are also a choice to get voters out. Being asked questions makes voters feel important and relevant to authorities. I have been sent various questionnaires before regarding my thoughts on jobs, the environment, what the candidate's top priority should be and how I would prefer tax money to be spent. This truly gave me a sense of belonging and power because I felt as if my views count and that candidates are not just asking for my vote but also my opinion. However, since candidates really rely on these surveys it is highly important for voters to be knowledgeable. They must possess facts about the issues they see as the top three. They must read books, articles and reliable newspapers. Only then can polling be worth the effort. For example, many voters still believe the reason we have so many people in prison is due to a high crime rate and that more and more criminals are arising every day. However, facts suggest that the real reason for packed prisons in America is longer and longer prison terms being assigned by judges.

If candidates follow the guidelines and attract voters by these legal and ethical methods, they are bound to succeed in the election even if they do not get elected. Candidates want to stand out but not for the bad reasons. Also, diversity in judges does not always guarantee fair sentencing. It is important to have more non-white people holding authority and top ranking positions; however, if the culture is not fixed, electing a non-white judge does not change anything in the system. Very few Americans know that we have a black judge on the Supreme Court. Clarence Thomas has been on board with many of the rulings Americans have been hurt by since 1991. Hillary Clinton was a woman and Secretary of State. She called for more war, more privacy intrusion, and rarely mentioned anything about the American criminal justice system being a threat. President

Obama was black. He witnessed the harshest treatment of unarmed African-Americans under his regime. The point is, if a culture of cruelty exists within any organization it does not matter who leads it because they too will come to believe that bribery is okay; the prison industry should be propped up; and social class should play a role in sentencing. They will absorb the culture and view women, African-Americans, Muslims… as less than human and worthy of degradation or be passive and accept the norm. Placing non-white people or women in high ranking positions does not change how corporate elites view these groups because on the other end cruelty is being taught to people who enter the system. The ideology must be replaced; not the person.

Voting will not remove all the flaws in our system. We must demand a clear interpretation and investigation into the 4th Amendment of our Constitution. We must examine the morality deficit in this country and realize that racism is not enough to explain cruelty by police, judges or prison officials. There is a bigger picture. If these officials were racist prior to their careers then they would never have made it so far up the system. Cruelty is involved. There exists a deeply imbedded pernicious view -- not a group of officers who have somehow made their way into the system. We must call for the collapse of the prison industry. After all, is "Let's Build Schools; Not Prisons" just a slogan?

# OUR FAMILY

In "Our Environment" I talked a lot about our connections and the social and environmental impact. This is supported by the criminological theory known as social disorganizational theory. Here, the setting is more relevant than individual characteristics or specific attributes related to the person. This theory suggests that people commit crimes not because they come from a certain background (like Islam) or due to the fact that they experience a medical condition (like Asperger's disease) alone. It emphasizes where we live; with who we mingle; are we employed or out of a decent job; do we have a loving family; and whether we feel needed in our community.

1 in 5 American children live solely with one parent. Our cage is being emptied and this does not help the next generation. It is true that Adam Lanza (the Connecticut school terrorist) was known to have mental instability and Asperger's disease but when we look at Lanza's environment we see that mental illness was not the only factor leading to his actions. His family made a major move from New Hampshire in 1998 that would define how his living conditions would be for the rest of his life. He changed many schools and his teachers were unable to keep him connected to the school community. His mental state, however, did not prevent him from learning. He would earn either A's or B's and move up similar to his other classmates. He attended college at age 16 but dropped out. My J.L.A. professor at W.C.S.U. said he would always earn an A on every test, project and homework. The only time he did get a

question wrong was when my professor had made a grammatical error in the question and every student in the class had got it wrong. Soon his parents would divorce and Lanza would have limited contact with his father. His mother had a passion for guns and would take Lanza to shooting ranges. Finally he stayed home for the rest of his life, alone without any reliable friends or a job. After this the result would not have been shocking had America known about what was missing in Lanza's cage.

In order to protect what is in our cage, especially the family, I believe a good method is exogamy. This not so typical way of meeting people can fix some of the cracks people see in their environment and allow them to transition into a new one. I am not just referring to a different race or a different culture; although that too sometimes opens doors to groups of people who maybe live in a better environment than we do due to their emphasis on the family, as an example or other variance in views. Some of us know that East Asian cultures are really respectful to their elderly. Maybe that means grandparents are more present in children's lives and therefore, provide that sense of belonging in a more efficient way than Western cultures do. Iranians are strict when it comes to their children's education. In the Iranian culture skipping college and higher education is a no no. Even if it means getting accepted to a private college where entry exams are eliminated you must attend college and graduate. Maybe that means children's education is better guaranteed and that if you are raised by an Iranian father for example, you are more likely to go to college. If you choose not to work in the same area as your major, it is excused.

However, there is also the financial side to exogamy. This may be harder to accomplish because of our environment yet there are methods to meet people who do not share the same address as we do; do not work at the same job as we do; and do not shop at the same places we do. The gated community has made this tougher and tougher every day. Those who are better off are isolating themselves from the rest of the population and creating class division and unintended segregation. This selfish view of the world has allowed for the poor to marry the poor; the rich to marry the rich; the drug addict to marry the drug addict; and the educated to marry the educated. It is even present in world geographies. Due to its area, economy and population California has been viewed as a candidate for possibly even considering seceding from the U.S. It houses some of the most rich and thriving corporations like Google, Apple and Microsoft. It has mostly been neoliberal in its political views and it contains some of the nation's most prestigious universities. For heaven's sake the movie and theater industry resides there! But the benefits do not last long. Kosovo and South Sudan are some of the regions President Clinton and President Obama promoted to divide and declare independence. Since their "victories" Kosovo has been labeled the most underdeveloped European nation as far as European standards go and the world's leader in heroin production while South Sudan has been battling hunger, migration and war. We believe in removing borders and limiting walls yet we have erected some of the most sturdy walls all throughout America and the world in the past 27 years.

When exogamy is practiced more people with poor environments can leave their lives of abuse, persecution, poverty, depression, addiction and loneliness to enter into an environment where there does exist a mother-in-law who can be looked at as the mother a young man never had. Where there does exist a career a high school drop-out can call empowering. Where there is a decent home not located in the slums. I am not promoting family-favoring or hiring people who possess zero qualifications but it is tradition in many other countries for managers of high end companies to bring their children, spouses, parents and even friends into the business. They see that their distant cousin has been out of a job for a long time and randomly assign them to various positions. We may not want that in this country but we can be more considerate of people who need to transition and change their lives. We could write that letter of rec-ommendation or agree to serve as a reference for someone who has no education but has been working in the hopes of a prestigious job. We could take a break from online shopping and visit the mall again and meet people we would never meet online. We could sell one of our three cars and take the bus to the gym and bring diversity to the station.

Americans even lack financial diversity among their group of friends. We find friends at the same school we study; the same job we work at; the same address we live; and the same places we shop. If you are a teacher there is a likely chance most of your friends are teachers too. If your parents have separated then most of your friends' parents have also separated. The trend needs to be lim-ited and the barriers need to come down. We need to see more places where diverse populations can meet and change their environments. We need to see more generalization rather than specification. As an example, I like to attend my local library. It's where I have been borrowing books since I was a child with my brother and I like to watch the new movies that come out on DVD that are available at the library for free as opposed to Netflix. Sometimes there are dis-carded books and movies available for the public to take home. There are even times when the library sells new items. Whenever I go there I rarely see anyone in their twenties borrowing books. Most clients are the elderly, the poor or mothers with their preschool chil-dren. Why has the library, a free government funded organization become a gathering spot for certain groups of people with certain characteristics? Why don't people from all walks of life regardless of their financial status or class or background join the library com-munity and provide that necessary setting for the uneducated, the poor, the abused and the lonely to change their environments and guarantee the existence of the family in the cage?

Think about the places a college professor might go to during the week. Would it include the rehabilitation center; a cafe; the social services department; or the grocery store? Maybe two of those places would fall into coincidence with a former criminal. Let's say the professor goes to the cafe and while waiting in line she starts a conversation with the person standing in front of her. The customer turns out to be a traffic violator with a criminal record and a single mother. After paying the bill the professor offers to recommend the customer to her university and encourages her to apply for adjunct professor. They trade phone numbers and turn out to become long-term friends. How did this occur? The cafe provided the opportunity for people from different walks of life to meet and change their environments for the better. The cafe was not segregated and attracted many people from the community regardless of their class, status, background, age and money. Now imagine a segregated world. A former drug addict meets a man on the bus who also used to have addiction and similar to the woman his parents have also separated. They talk and end up meeting each other every day at the station. They get married and live a life of poverty because no employer ever trusts them with work. This brings them a sense of alienation and hopelessness and they start using drugs for a second time after many years of abstinence. How did this happen? Public transportation was categorized for certain groups of people living in the community, therefore making the chances of meeting someone without a life of addiction very rare. It helped the addicted to remain addicted.

Unlike the library, public transportation is not free, which makes me wonder how could it have become segregated and a way of life for specific people with specific features such as former addicts; the poor; old people who do not drive anymore; and sadly, prostitutes. In Connecticut, in order to take the bus you must pay $1.75 per person. So even if you are homeless you still have to be able to afford $3.50 to go to and from your destination. This is not cheap yet the rich still refuse to fund and use public services. I do not have my own car. I rely on my family to drive me but if only the bus would stop at my house I would not wait on my dad for a ride. I see bus stations planted at locations where no one ever stands and waits. There are no businesses near them and no houses. I have even seen bus stops near the highway where weeds have invested in empty lands. There are far too rarely actual stations where passengers can sit and avoid the rain or stand. Mostly it is rather just a pole or a bus sign that indicates a bus stops here, if you were wondering.

Brooke King is a veteran of the Iraq war. She left to join the battle right when Saddam was still in power and the whole world had turned against him. She describes the horrors and violence of the war in her autobiography titled "War Flower." Immoral acts by generals; losing friends; being shot; and most importantly the struggles after leaving war that start to show up. In the middle of all that violence she describes meeting the man of her dreams at a base in Kuwait. She says Kuwait was worse than Iraq, the actual place where the war took place. They were both college drop-outs and both had lived through the war environment. They planned on getting married after their return to America but the marriage did not last (not surprised). King had Post Traumatic Stress Disorder and had attempted suicide during her marriage. She had constant nightmares and the war scenes would not leave her alone. Her husband on the other hand had trouble finding work and had turned to drugs as a source of help. King's husband committed suicide years later. How did this happen? Two people who shared the same background decided to meet each other. A veteran met another veteran instead of someone from a different background, for instance, someone who has never been to war and has no military experience. How could someone who has experienced violence help someone else who has also experienced war and guns and soldiers dying right in front of his eyes? There is no chance for either of them to transition into an environment where violence is unknown, stress is limited, and help is transferable from person to person.

In his book "Palaces for the People," Eric Klinenberg criticizes the disappearance of settings and locations dedicated to both rich populations and poor populations. He says that not even libraries are getting enough funding for the poor, mothers and the elderly to meet. (It is worth mentioning I borrowed his book from the library instead of purchasing it from Amazon.) Malls are shutting down due to online competition and parks are not well kept. America's leading shopping retailers such as Sears, J.C. Penny and Toys R. Us have filed for bankruptcy. The chances of meeting someone from a different environment just turned from zero to negative. Department stores are a totally American idea. They were developed when America was investing in itself, therefore department stores are somehow part of our culture now. Klinenberg calls these places social infrastructure: physical places and organizations that shape the way people interact. His focus is less on the segregation of neighborhoods, schools, buses or restaurants but rather highlights the fact that not even rich people can meet rich people because there is a lack of physical space. The internet is the suspect and more and more people regardless of their status are gathering there instead of social infrastructure. Universities are in decline making the likelihood of even educated people to meet educated people rare. Students are studying online which reduces school funding for various physical programs and face to face classes. The anti-taxing ideology has added to the disappearance of social infrastructure in such a way that new schools, parks, libraries or even restaurants are never built not even for the poor.

As I mentioned, the benefits of breaking off do not last. Take a look at our celebrities. They are not even called artists anymore; or were they ever? They have become a class of their own and have separated themselves from ordinary citizens. How many actors, singers, TV personalities and directors should I name who were rich; had lots of fame; lived in large homes; were friends with other famous people; and traveled all around the world who eventually committed suicide? Art is the most alienated career in America. When we decide to call people celebrities instead of artists it puts them into a different category than the rest of the population. They walk around with bodyguards while regular people are more likely to face rape or terror. They hide their faces with hats and sunglasses. These acts have more consequences for them than their fans. The fans have also helped with their alienation by intentionally treating them differently. They run after a famous actor when they see him or her doing their daily routine just like everyone else in society. They scream and want to take pictures. Their love and interest in the actor has made the actor seem like they are worth being above society. That Hollywood should be a class of its own as if it is some saint from heaven.

Some academic scholars and scientists believe that if we construct social infrastructure that is meant for the rich, the educated and people who are not alienated in places where the poor, the elderly, and former criminals live then we can reduce segregation and provide space for diverse groups to connect. This however, has proven to not be the case when we observe reality. Yale University is the most prestigious and popular university world-wide. Many people from other countries come to study at Yale and spend thousands of dollars just to have a Yale education. However, New Haven the city where Yale is located is one of the most defunded cities of Connecticut. It has a 3.8 unemployment rate and only 35% of residents have a bachelor's degree or higher. When I visit the city sometimes I see acres and acres of land that is left abandoned by former factories that once provided thousands of jobs for residents. The buildings are not only empty, they also provide an ugly view to the city and a sense of neglect. The students who attend Yale are mostly not from New Haven. 196 new students who entered Yale in 2018 were from New York; 187 were from California; and 201 students were from outside of the country. Among the new students who were from Connecticut (118) most were not from New Haven. Yale has a 5.6% black student population yet 33% of New Haven residents are black, meaning we cannot guarantee that this 5.6% even includes black New Haveners. Therefore, even though a university is located in a city where the poor and the uneducated live, it is as if it is still segregated and does not exist at all because the poor cannot make it into the university. It is still a place dedicated to the educated and better off. Financial aid is available yet New Haven residents cannot study at Yale because of family expectations and work.

A similar situation exists with places meant for the poor, the addicted, and the alienated. Just because a prison facility is located in your neighborhood it does not equal to residents of that neighborhood being involved with the prison system. In fact, the facility may be situated in a gated community or somewhere in the pricy areas of Manhattan, New York, however, the prisoners are from out of state. They are not from Manhattan or even the state of New York. They could be from Vermont or Connecticut which means location does not matter when talking about segregation of restaurants, schools, parks, transportation, housing and work. The poor, the uneducated, the addicted and the alienated need to be able to walk into those infrastructures to be able to connect with someone who does not share the same background as they. This could happen even if the facility is not located near their address.

In their book, "Poor Economics" Abhijit Banerjee and Esther Duflo talk about poverty in developing countries and the various programs their governments and global organizations have dedicated to helping the poor step out of their lives of financial struggles. They travel to East Asia only to find that lacking a decent job or going out of business is not the only reason people become poor. Many people in India or Bangladesh seem to also possess certain behaviors that keep them poor in addition to their financial situation. For example, the authors noticed doctors, teachers and other professions come to work whenever they want and leave whenever they want. There are no rules to commit workers to their roles. Immunizations and vaccines are available with incentives, however, families still neglect taking their children to get the process done. They have TVs, cellphones and various forms of entertainment at home yet cannot afford to buy food because entertainment is also a need. They have multiple children in the hopes of at least two or one of them becoming successful. These behaviors are no different than a high school dropout meeting a high school dropout or a businessman meeting a businesswoman in America or Canada. The authors also found out in their research that there are ways to change people's behaviors. In Brazil for instance, many TV series have changed the way people decide on the number of children to have. The actors in Brazilian TV shows typically have one child or no children at all. They are portrayed as very different than the average Brazilian citizen; however, this has been for the better. American TV on the other hand has not helped change endogamy or promote exogamy. Many of the shows and series on Hallmark or HBO channels mirror the average American. Actors are divorced; they have addiction; they cannot afford a living; and worst of all they approve of the behaviors we are suffering from such as meeting people at the same locations we work, study, shop and live. There is no other way for the viewer to think that maybe going to the library does not necessarily mean I am a dedicated reader. Maybe taking the bus can be fun and reduce my car expenses. The only time an actor is shown taking public transportation is when he or she lives in the city and therefore, owning a car is less likely. There is no point of reference. I am not saying TV is the only method to improve where we meet people or make friends. In fact, TV does not have the same meaning it once did. My family spends the most time watching Roku and other applications that work with the internet. However, even among those programs there exist few chances for people to step out of their usual methods and change their behaviors. If we are acting the same way as people in East Asia or Brazil then what is the difference between a developed country and a developing country? To the credit of countries like India or Indonesia there still exist connections over there. People do not feel as alienated as Americans or Canadians. As I said, grandparents are more involved. Education is a must. Their culture can be a way out for their bad behaviors but what about us? Even if a young Bangladeshi girl grows up poor she still has the opportunity to marry a rich boy when she gets older because her parents will enforce it. They will not allow her to marry anyone she wants. In America, our parents have a limit as to who they can tell us to start a relationship with. We can choose whomever we want but isn't odd that so often we choose the wrong person?

The next tip is for work to be more family friendly in America. The amount of money we pay for day-care and preschool is alarming at this moment. Alabama reports over $400 per month for child care. Other states report over $900. Why can't we take care of our own children? My solution is for day-cares to be prevalent at the workplace and work schedules to be more considerate of parent employees. At Western Connecticut State University there was a preschool set up on campus for students and professors to leave their children while they attended class. I think if the facility did not exist most of the parent students would abandon their education and the professors would become stay-at-home mothers. If we are committed to workers' rights this should be the number one priority of human rights advocates and activists. We should not fear losing our jobs or staying out of work. This is a basic right and we have the money to sponsor it.

It may seem shocking, but in America we still do not operate on equal pay. Congress passed the Equal Pay Act in 1963 which made it illegal for employers private and public to pay less to female workers when they in fact share the same responsibilities, duties, and hardships of the job with male workers. There has been much additional legislation since then, yet somehow women are not making as much money as men. Women led households are on the rise. Stay at home fathers are becoming a new reality and this means women definitely need some push in their finances to pay the bills. Forbes says this is because there exist many disparities in how female workers in whatever field promote their work; public trust in women run businesses; gender bias; and the prevalence of female suited jobs. Therefore, legally we do not have wage discrimination. Our main problem is how women themselves can keep up in the job industry and grab attention. For example, my parents used to for a long time believe that male doctors were more knowledgeable and capable in their position than female doctors. They used to take my brother and I to mostly male pediatricians and eye doctors, however that belief faded once we grew up and started contacting our own doctors. My parents realized their great work and started going to female doctors themselves. Such examples reduce the likelihood of women being able to make the same amount of money as men. When all patients choose to visit male doctors how could a female doctor make the same amount of money as the male doctor when she does not even have the same number of clients even though there exist equal pay laws?

In many Muslim countries female run taxi cabs are in style. That is, they are not just run by female employees but rather the drivers are all women and they only offer service to female passengers. They are color coded in either purple or have a sign on the top of the vehicle indicating it is a female service. This is an example of creating jobs suitable for women. Even in our own New York City I never rode with a female taxi driver. There literally still exist jobs that lack female representation but not in the sense that we think. This is acceptable in some circumstances because for example, women cannot climb electric power lines. They cannot control forklifts or heavy operating machines. It is physically impossible and that is fine. Some of these jobs women do not even like to be involved in such as football. We do not have a female football team even though we have female soccer teams, basketball teams, bowling teams… In order to make equal pay work there have to be jobs that are meant for women next to the jobs that are not gender based such as medical, education, law and banking. Yet even in these jobs women need to stand out and provide good advertising because there is competition with male candidates. We have many female based hair salons and beauty parlors that solely provide service to women. We have of course gynecologists that are meant for female patients anyway. These jobs are not segregation; they widen the range of job availability and allow women to stand out. They create a market catering to a certain population, however they do not reduce the chances of meeting someone from a different environment. It is basically a form of business.

The Family & Medical Leave Act was perhaps the most the government ever did for American families. It allowed for mothers of new born children to take time off from work for 12 months while still being able to preserve their careers. Also, employees with family concerns or relatives with medical conditions can benefit from this law as well. This is regardless of whether one works at a private institution or public organization. However, even this can be furthered. The Family & Medical Leave Act does not guarantee a salary and paid time off. Mothers who have just started a family are struggling with finances and bills. On one hand they have child expenses, on the other hand they must keep up with groceries, electricity and rent. My suggestion is to refine the deal and add paid time off for workers. The Pregnancy Discrimination Act was one family rights policy that was furthered through the courts. (A good example of laws and amendments being made through unelected judges; however, this was for the better.) In Young vs. United Parcel Service a pregnant worker was unable to lift heavy boxes and packages yet when she asked her boss for a lighter load he refused and told Pat Young to leave her job. Originally, the Act banned the firing of pregnant workers but after Young vs. U.P.S. it was revised to include pregnant workers on the list of disabled employees. That is, Young should have been treated as a worker with a disability such as someone in a wheelchair or missing limb and that her boss had no right to fire her. This was a victory for worker's rights and family rights.

Johann Hari emphasized the need for connections to exist. If we disconnect from the family and fail to add programs and policies that support this essential ingredient in our cage we will be looking for substitutes that will surely not satisfy our needs in a healthy life. We will be searching and searching without a clear understanding of what we need that used to be right there in the cage but is now missing due to some life event like our parents' divorce or a job loss. Next to the programs, we also need to change our behavior. This is not controlled by a politician or lobbyist; thankfully. Addiction, abuse, divorced parents and under education are not things to have in common with someone. They are not like our favorite music or our favorite food. Only someone who lives in a full cage can lift someone else out of alienation and introduce them to a new environment. They can share their parents, their career their home and their traditions with someone who has all of these missing and feels alienated as a result. Perhaps it is better to move out of our comfort zone. Take a look at where we are before we decide to meet someone. For example, is it a rehabilitation center or the cafe?

Our lives are becoming too predictable. We need to create spaces where diverse populations can meet and connect regardless of their status. We have all heard of people who enjoy saying they are the first ones in their family to go to college. How many of those people do we personally know? How prevalent is that story which corporations constantly remind us of regardless of what reality is? Many are also the first to not go in their family. Diversity is not just in appearance; it is also in lifestyles, family, friends, work and money. We need to also demand better conditions for parent workers and not fear losing our jobs. It is undemocratic for us to make our people choose between preserving their family or keeping their job. Work and family are both required in the cage. If one is eliminated the other will be at risk.

# THERE IS A LEGAL WAY AROUND THE BORDER

At this time it is impossible to talk about immigration without talking about jobs. It is as if they are the same subject now and somehow intertwined. When I visited Toronto I could not help but notice the advertising and large billboards surrounding Yonge Street. The entire road is covered with successful Iranian businesses who have managed to either open restaurants, supermarkets, attorney offices or real estate agencies. My family and I ate at the restaurants, stopped at currency exchange and even shopped at the local Khorak Supermarket. I could say it is as large as an Aldi supermarket and has all the foods popular among Iranians, Arabs, Afghans and Turks. Many Muslims also look to Khorak to provide them with their *halal* meat. The signs and slogans were even written in Persian next to the English. There are also plenty of Iranian doctors and medical physicians in Toronto. Their ads run through the Persian language magazines and newspapers.

I think immigrants can make great contributions if they stay focused on why they have left their home countries and what their main goal was in migration. Immigrants come in various shapes and forms. There is not just one characteristic with which to associate them. For example, they do not all speak Spanish and they do not all follow Islam. There may be a common population such as in Canada

*Iranian businesses, lawyers, doctors and real estate through "Atash" newspaper*

where most immigrants seemed to be from Asia. We rarely saw anyone from Mexico, Ecuador or Peru which are more common in America. However, there are other groups who co-exist. Immigrants can even be white or Native American. For instance, the student I teach English to is from Albania; a rare source. She is white, Muslim and has almost 10 years of experience as a kindergarten teacher. She has a master's degree in Cultural Heritage and is hoping to become a substitute teacher in America. She feels very homesick and talks to her parents every day through Skype and other video applications and it makes me feel sad too. Immigrants' reasons for migration are also varied. I personally believe if people are being haunted by terrorism, genocide, war or natural disasters they have every right to claim refuge in a neighboring country or somewhere farther away. However, this does not mean that we cannot control our immigration flow and design legal methods to not only end the chaos but also be more fair to people seeking America as their destination. People who take legal measures and apply for visas get denied most of the time. They spend thousands of dollars. They wait long years before they are notified that their visa is ready. Due to political disputes, our embassy does not operate in countries like Iran. That means Iranians who want to emigrate to America must first spend thousands of dollars and make a trip to neighboring Turkey or the United Arab Emirates and hand in their documents to our embassies there. When President Trump threatened to kick out illegal immigrants, many LEGAL immigrants feared losing their status. People who had moved to America in the 1980s, 1990s and 2000s and were living with green cards for decades rushed to apply for citizenship. From October 2016 through June 2017, 783,330 legal immigrants applied to become American citizens after so many years living as permanent residents. There was nothing wrong with their status and they did have documents, however the political mood was the main reason for their decision. There are many struggles and anyone who is rational would say it is not fair. Revising our Visa Waiver Program could be one step to more fairness.

Currently the program comprises 39 countries that do not require Americans applying for visas before making their travel. The same is expected of citizens of those countries when visiting America. When I looked at the list I was taken aback by the bias upon which the program was created. Of the 39 countries, 33 are located in Europe with the addition of Australia as a Western nation. Chile is the only South American nation on the list while Africa and West Asia have no representation at all. It is not clear exactly what are the requirements for becoming a member of the V.W.P. but I am sure whatever they are at least some Arab, Latin or African countries would be qualified to participate. A member of the BRICS countries South Africa has one the best economic situations on the continent with a $349 billion Gross Domestic Product and has friendly relations with America as far as politics go. Nigeria is even better with

$376 billion but is not so close in ideology when it comes to politics. Many of the Mediterranean countries also possess potential and are in fact caught up in some of the most harsh conditions of migration themselves. The United Nations Refugee Agency reports Turkey being the number one host to refugees currently in the entire globe. No Western nation has been able to make a similar claim at this point. Over 3 million Syrian migrants with legitimate reasons are seeking help in neighboring Turkey. A problem for which we are responsible. In fact, people whose lives are in danger are more likely to settle in neighboring countries rather than Western countries. Brazil is probably the most developed country in South America which also happens to be one of the emerging economies. It has a diverse population similar to our people and has been able to show itself off in some of the most popular events in the world such as hosting the World Cup. It has an area of 3.2 million square miles making it almost as big as the U.S. In fact, we have just as much in common with South America as we have with Europe. Some of them may not be so favorable such as colonization but Americans can definitely relate to citizens of Brazil, Argentina, Paraguay or the Caribbean. Most of these countries follow *jus soli*; which is the birth requirement for citizenship. European countries on the other hand follow *jus sanguinis*; which is the blood requirement for citizenship and in fact most of the world affiliates with it. Not even the European Union identifies with *jus soli*. Other similarities are in religion and language. Belize, Jamaica and the Bahamas speak English as their official language; unlike the popular belief which is Spanish. Many of the former Communist countries have also risen in the past 27 years even though many neoliberals like Joe Biden would rather deny it and pretend Russia is still the Soviet Union; Cuba is still Castro and China lives in the Mao years. That ideology is simply not corelated to reality because globalization has not allowed it. Many of the countries we know as dictatorships have in fact been forced to open up even if it was against their will. For instance, almost every head of state or world leader nowadays has a Facebook or Twitter account. Social media use to be banned in Iran or Russia but now even Vladimir Putin has a Twitter page. When President Obama was in office he put effort into lifting sanctions on Cuba and normalizing relations. This is what the people need over there and perhaps such efforts could easily reduce illegal migration as well. When people are able to live better lives in their native countries they are less likely to make the move and emigrate. If you really want to know what it is like to live under sanctions just ask Iran and Venezuela. These two countries have had high levels of migration and people cannot afford to buy anything. They have been cut off from doing business with major economies and can only rely on everyone's friend: China. President Trump once questioned why America does not have many immigrants from Norway. Well, if one were to look at economic, cultural, political, social and educational life in Norway in comparison to Cuba, Haiti, Pakistan or Iran the answer would become pretty obvious.

The V.W.P. could be a perfect opportunity to also look for allies that are closer to us geographically. Since the first Cold War we have been searching for friends who live thousands of miles away from us while ignoring the very countries that are located nearby. It is definitely important to have allies in all parts of the world but we have completely stopped searching in South America. The number of times our presidents have met with Arab leaders private and public cannot be compared to the number of times they have sat down with Latin leaders. In fact, the media rarely covers any economic, political, cultural or social treaties we sign with South American countries. The only time they do report on relations between the Americas is when the human rights industry is involved and there is talk about illegal immigration. In fact, this lack of communication is one reason we have not been able to resolve illegal immigration; not even with our next door neighbor Mexico, a transit country. Many of the countries we claim are a threat have in fact very good relations with their next door neighbors and their neighbors do not share our view while being more than just two. For example, Iran, a heavily embargoed country has managed to conduct economic relations with Turkey, Iraq, Armenia, Azerbaijan, Turkmenistan, Afghanistan and Pakistan. All of these countries live next to Iran and they have never claimed Iran being a threat while we live thousands of miles away and always seem to claim Iran is a threat. They are also diverse: Armenia is Christian; Turkey, Azerbaijan and Turkmenistan are Sunni; while Afghanistan and Pakistan reside in Central Asia. All of these countries also speak varied languages. North Korea while hostile to South Korea has always managed to be influenced politically by China, for the better. Its economy heavily depends of China as well. We need to focus more on New World relations rather than American-Arab relations, American-Euro relations or American-Asian relations. There is a lot of potential and shared characteristics among the Americas which we have chosen to walk right past.

If the V.W.P. is expanded it would help bring fairness to the immigration process in such a way that illegal migration would be reduced and diversity would be more visible in the program. For instance, why would an Ecuadorian citizen decide to make a long trip to North America when he or she could easily take the legal route without needing a visa? This would significantly reduce the illegal resident population in America and provide steps for them to become green card holders and eventually citizens. They would be able to live more productive lives and better fulfill their intentions for migrating to another country.

Perhaps the best thing that comes out of this is an end to cheap labor. Illegal immigrants get taken advantage of and are banned from many benefits and insurance. They are paid lower wages and cannot stand up for their rights because they are illegal. They do not wish to risk their jobs or their presence in America so they abide by the unfair rules. I am shocked by the fact that no

N.G.O. has ever called out maltreatment by major companies and employers. Their behavior goes against the Immigration Reform & Control Act of 1986. Under this law, American companies and employers are forbidden to hire immigrants who have missing documents, fraudulent documents, or no documents at all. There are heavy fines and sanctions imposed against employers who hire illegal immigrants. We have not been notified of any American company shutting down or going to court, however.

Towards the end of the first Cold War, Congress passed the Immigration Act of 1990. This was when emigration from former Communist countries was going to be very high. In this there are many employment categories such as investors, highly educated immigrants; skilled labor, and special immigrants which mostly refers to those with specific career options such as clerics. Each of the categories has its own requirements even skilled labor. According to the Act, skilled labor immigrants must possess two years of training or experience in order to be qualified for a visa. Therefore, even if an immigrant has entered the country legally they must still have had work experience and knowledge of a job. Visas cannot be granted to foreigners who have never worked in their own country yet many immigrants today are in fact in the skilled labor force in America without prior knowledge of the subject in their home country. That is, we see immigrants working in factories, construction, department stores and hotels without having the skilled labor visa and adherence to the Immigration Act of 1990. They may be living here legally, however they arrived under a different form of visa such as fiancé or for medical reasons. This is why my second proposal would be to limit immigrant employment to education required jobs. This does not necessarily mean we should only submit visas to college educated migrants or doctors and engineers. An immigrant with no education at all can be qualified for entry but there will be no skills required jobs available for them once they reach here. They would need to apply to college or some kind of certificate program in order to occupy a position in the medical field, education, business, marketing, the arts and law.

With two branches in Waterbury and Danbury, Connecticut, Naugatuck Valley Community College lists a wide range of Associate and Certificate programs on its website. Every area from digital arts, economics and paralegal to social work, nursing and philosophy is present. They even educate in the field of aviation and flight. Their associates degree in Aviation Science Management is a short two-year program and perhaps the most eye catching on the list. With a requirement of just 62 credits the study covers two math classes, one English Literature class, two general physics courses and one computer course. The rest is dedicated to aviation itself plus one general psychology class. These are also transferable to top universities in the country and can be used to earn a bachelor's degree in the future. On the bottom of the page there is a fascinating list of what students in Aviation Science Management can do once they graduate. Flight attendants earn as much as $23.75 per hour. Air Field Operations Specialists can earn $28.94 an hour. Other possibilities include airport authority, commercial airlines and working as agents for the Federal Aviation Administration or National Transportation Safety Board.

Among their certificate degrees N.V.C.C. has some of the best options that are not only low cost but also short and time efficient if you are a parent or needed in the family full-time. The Certified Nursing Aide or Medical Assistant is probably the most prestigious option as far as certification goes. It does not require a high school diploma and costs just $1,500 for the entire educational experience. Textbooks are provided when tuition is paid and training is involved alongside classroom instruction. C.N.A.s draw blood, take vital signs, perform injections, ask health questions and prepare the clinic before the doctor arrives to see the patient. Their role is crucial to the medical team and they are relied upon for assistance.

The second option for immigrants could be promoting their mother tongue. They could be leading the language departments of our high schools and even introduce new languages to the school system such as Persian, Mandarin, Hebrew, Portuguese, Aymara and many of the native languages of South America. This is knowledge immigrants already possess and do not need to acquire at a university or educational institute. My high school taught Spanish, French and German as foreign language options for students to take. There were two French teachers and one German teacher yet while there were over five Spanish teachers very few were of Spanish descent or Mestizo, (people of European and Native American heritage). That to me is kind of odd when we have such a large Latin population in America. Immigrants could even look into college programs and promote their culture through the African Studies, Latin Studies and Asian Studies programs. Many Muslims would be offered the chance to reveal the real image of Islam instead of what the status quo teaches people about it. Is it not interesting to learn about a culture through the voice of a native instead of a second party?

At W.C.S.U. many of my professors were immigrants. My West Asian studies professor was from Libya and he used to talk all the time about how he escaped the country after the coup. He said he was a diplomat and that Ghadafi was after him for political reasons. He was very detailed when teaching about Islam. Sometimes I would criticize him because the class was probably a first for many students and so they may not have been ready for learning how to do daily prayers or the importance of the cleanliness of the area you pray. Overall the students liked him and rarely anyone missed his class. He spoke five languages and was very particular. He said that rarely does anyone in Libya speak only one language. Most people speak either Arabic and French or Arabic and English or all three! My Politics of Poverty professor on the other hand was from Turkey. He always criticized President Erdogan and his involvement with terror. He was able to challenge many of the students' popular beliefs regarding imperialism and neocolonialism and expose them to how foreign hands are involved in many of the region's crises. Many Native Americans of the South could also promote Mayan and Aztec culture. Unfortunately, I did not have any Ecuadorian or Colombian professors which is a shame when we have so many people from South America. There are many opportunities when we look to education for an answer to a better life.

The American soccer team ranks 22nd on the official list of FIFA rankings in the world. The South American countries that lead the top ten are Brazil, Uruguay, Argentina and Colombia. Soccer is another field where immigrants especially from South America or Mexico can lead the way and raise the American team up to global standards. They could not only live the American Dream but also make soccer in America more prevalent and a popular sport. They could multiply sponsors and donors for the teams and make American soccer the talk of the day. There could be a possibility for American youth to run home for the next soccer game that is on instead of football. In fact, very few American soccer players in history have been of Spanish origin. Landon Donovan, Clint Dempsey and Abby Wambach are among the most famous when we talk about soccer in America. We could use immigrant potential to lift soccer in America and bring it up to the same level as countries like Brazil or Argentina. It would be quite a surprise to hear of America winning its first ever World Cup!

Is it not an immigrant's dream to be able to succeed in a country where opportunities are plenty and reaching your goals is supposed to be more real? We are home to some of the best universities and institutes in the world. We have financial aid available. Would it be racism to call for immigrants to make more money, live in better neighborhoods and have their children attend better schools? Once this is accomplished skilled labor would be prevalent for Americans seeking to work in factories or other blue collar jobs.

Although this does not remove the technology threat to labor, it can help reduce outside influence over American jobs and provide a fair balance for those who want to grow and live better lives and those who want to share a country with full potential.

In his book, *Capitalism, Alone* Branco Milanovic talks about some major changes that need to occur in the globalist agenda. Some have already occurred by rising countries like China, Malaysia and Indonesia, where state capitalism rules the country or in Iran where religion is tightly tied to capitalist policies. Countries are replacing the globalism in capitalism and using their own methods to conduct it. This phenomenon is a major part of Cold War II. Next to this Milanovic also brings up another form of change: immigration policies. He says if immigrants are not exactly equal to citizens of that particular country then the citizens are more likely to accept them even if their numbers are high. He brings up some policies that are already underway such as permanent residency. Permanent residents are green card holders who were previously on visa. People who are permanent residents can do many of the activities citizens are able to do such as obtain a driver's license; apply to school or college; apply for financial aid; buy a house; get a job; travel in and out of the country; and marry citizens of the country they live in (which changes their status to citizen). They can basically do anything citizens are able to do except vote and apply for political positions. Milanovic says racism is also limited when there exists a line between citizen and immigrant. However, there are consequences for the immigrants themselves. They may feel different or alienated such as immigrants do in France, one of the main countries exporting terrorists to West Asia. France has an anti-religion policy known as *lacite* which restricts people from showing religious affiliation in public. This has been an issue for Muslims who want to wear scarves, veils and other types of *hijab* around the city. In France, many Muslims are segregated without intent; that means they feel different and cannot connect to the French population not because of a particular law but because of the inability of the French government to reform immigration. They have friends who are mostly of the same ethnic group as they are and live in their own neighborhood. But placing restrictions on immigrant careers would only work for the better as opposed to placing restrictions on their status or religious rights. I am calling for immigrants to work more prestigious and higher paying jobs than citizens so there should be no room for alienation or feeling like an outsider.

I believe as long as we are involved in world affairs, as long as we are bombing other countries, as long as we grow our military bases and sponsor coups in the Caribbean or Arab world we are not allowed to close our borders to anyone. We owe the people who come here from Iran, Venezuela, Mexico, Iraq, Somalia and many more places where our footprints are visible. Few Americans know we are now involved in 10 wars. It is not just Afghanistan and Iraq anymore. My Comparative Politics professor at W.C.S.U. covered an entire lesson on immigration in France. She mentioned how the French feel attacked by the rising number of Arabs and that racism is starting to take hold because they fear losing French identity and all the customs associated with it such as language, *lacite,* sports and holidays. My professor tried to explain it to us using simpler things like how the French love their cheese and their bread. When I thought about it more deeply, I realized she was talking about traditions. Maybe they should have thought about this when they were colonizing vast areas of Africa or more recently conducting the coup in Libya through NATO. Africa acts the same as South America for the U.S. It is located just below the European continent and many Arabs and Africans try to enter Europe illegally similar to how the Spanish try to enter North America. Their situation is no different than Mestizos in America.

Yet we are allowed to promote lawfulness, control and limitation in order to bring fairness, responsibility and end chaos. This should not seem as harsh to anyone who believes in native rights

*Colonialism such as French occupation of Africa and neocolonialism such as sponsorship of coups are the main reasons for people leaving their homes. This could be legally or illegally.*

and immigrant rights in tandem. America believes in co-existence; not replacing a group of people with another group of people. That was what we did during colonization. That would only bring alienation and disconnect for people who were born here and know the culture, traditions and language. We witness the results every day. A young man starts shooting inside a mosque, a Jewish temple or is hostile toward Sikhs due to some distorted belief. Is racism and hate really enough to explain his behavior? I talked about this in "Our Environment" and "Our Family." Some of our holidays are fading from our cage. Put this next to the fact that this young man's family has also disappeared and he is jobless. What happens next affects us all. We don't celebrate Christmas just because we are Christian. In fact, some of us do not even go to church the morning of Christmas. We don't value Thanksgiving solely because our parents celebrate it and therefore, it has been passed down to us like our hair color. We don't hold Valentine's Day because we have a duty and obligation to keep the spirit alive for years and years to come. We have these things because they give us purpose and welcoming. They make us feel we are part of something. In fact, it would be interesting to know that many non-Christians are celebrating Christmas in America. They do not feel offended as the status-quo would like to presume when we say "Merry Christmas" or "Happy Easter." Many immigrants today are celebrating Thanksgiving and Independence Day; two of the most American holidays. This is against popular belief and we can be more vocal about these peaceful, joyous and needed traditions.

Caleb Cain is a former far-right terrorist. He started purchasing guns after being drowned in various YouTube propaganda and hateful Neo-Nazi videos. He believed Muslims are taking over Western culture and that there needs to be a stop to their actions before the white population is a minority. YouTube, Facebook, Twitter and Google are some of the most common places where Alt-Right radicals like Cain, the San Bernardino terrorist, the Las Vegas terrorist and many ISIS recruits look to for purpose and belonging. Cain's environment reminds me of Adam Lanza. A smart college drop-out; without a job; full time video gamer and a young boy in his twenties. Since he did not have a mental condition and was not Muslim he was labeled as racist and a hater by the media.

He was lost after high school and even before his graduation started showing signs of alienation and social isolation. He failed to connect with anyone but the internet. Why are psychologists not focusing on these environmental factors? Why are commentators so interested in three main categories: The person is either mentally ill; a Muslim; or right wing racist. The public never gets fed any different than these three categories. There is never any word of how he was raised; how many friends he had; whether he had gone through some tough life experiences or if he was unemployed. The talk of the day is always about personal traits like white or Asian; immigrant or American; mentally ill or sane; and Muslim or non-Muslim.

*Muslim perpetrators are always labeled as "terrorists" while Christian perpetrators are always called "the shooter." This is when both people suffer from the same environmental impacts and alienation.*

I do not fall for the common categories. Those are against social disorganizational theory and focus on the person's traits such as ethnicity instead of his living conditions and environment. I am against labeling theory. Personal traits like Arabic sounding names do not help us in figuring out why people commit crimes. Racism does not cover the bigger picture. Had Cain been at work full-time would he have had so much free time to dedicate to video games and YouTube trash? How come Muslims cannot be mentally ill? Are they vaccinated against Asperger's syndrome or any other type of mental disability? Muslim suspects are always labeled as "terrorists" yet when a Christian commits the same crime and ends up killing more people than the Muslim he is always labeled as "the shooter." John Earnest attacked a synagogue in San Diego, California. Similar to Cain, Lanza, Farook and McVeigh he was well educated and was studying nursing at California State University. He had a 4.3 GPA in high school and was involved in many school activities. After the tragic event at the synagogue he was not called a terrorist. Instead his actions were called "hate crimes." Similar to Farook who pledged allegiance to ISIS; Earnest pledged allegiance to the Alt-Right. How is ISIS and Al-Nusra propaganda different than what the Alt-Right post on YouTube; the same media outlet used by both groups? Do you remember Charlie from R.I. International? He was drowning in something similar and was disconnected from anything that had to do with family, work, friends, traditions and a sense of purpose. That led him to drugs and biker clubs. For Cain and Earnest, it was not drugs or biker clubs; it was the Alt-Right.

# TAMING THE NEW LEVIATHAN

In this book I tried to dedicate each chapter to at least one real life, tangible and recognizable issue we face in America. I tried to outline the real threats we face like where we put our money; how we need faith; defunding education and the growing carceral state. I did not need the all too famous "war on..." to make a statement to my fellow friends, neighbors, teachers and coworkers. That title is perhaps needed when we try to sell fictional issues to our people; when a threat is not so recognizable and is laying helpless for attention. When it needs to be magnified by the politically motivated media and sent out in a large envelope to each American household in order to get funded.

You probably already knew the details of each chapter once you read the title. You do not need someone to tell you what you are struggling with when you are the one experiencing the struggle. Why do we get updated every day on what the issues of the time are when we are present and alive and can see the issues with our own eyes? Only something that is invisible would need sirens, flashing lights and a big CAUTION sign. I did not need those for the topics in this book.

My hope is that after this era we can move on to fixing these real issues and suspend funding for the issues that are hard to relate to. We could afford funding for day-care at the workplace. We could add life skills to our education. There will be a plethora of money available once we decide to focus on the real issues. I would even call for the shutdown of some of the most obsolete agencies such as the Department of Homeland Security. Created with the intention of fighting terror it has proven to be weak and incompetent on real issues like natural disasters, viral diseases and other emergencies. In his book "Chasing Phantoms," Michael Barkun points out a disturbing incident during the time hurricane Katrina hit and how the Federal Emergency Management Agency handled it. The book focuses on how we are fighting unclear enemies and dedicating large amounts of money in order to destroy them. Disasters are plenty but we continue to search and analyze our lives. We install more cameras; hire more security guards; do more background checks yet we still have not found the devil. Barkun says when FEMA officials got to the scene they were talking about fighting terror and how the government needs to exceed funding for finding terrorists before they find us. This was in front of a large crowd of people who had just lost their homes, their memories and their loved ones to a storm.

America is not a poor country. We are not landlocked. We have many natural resources and we have a huge population. There is no acceptable reason for us not to be able to fix these issues. There is potential and we have history to prove it. Everyday people are working hard and making a difference in whatever area they are focused. No one is slacking or looking for a free ride. That is neoliberal propaganda. How can someone who has a criminal background be qualified as slacking when no company or employer ever gives them a chance? Charlie, the Peer Support Coach will never have any other form of career in his entire life. He has been committed to a better life; however, President Trump is busy expanding the war industry to space -- a $700 million project. How can parents be looked at as not working hard when they are cutting time from their families and a home cooked meal in order to work two jobs?

I believe everyone in this nation is committed, trying and giving it their everything to reach a better life. If we are struggling it is because manufactured issues are in the way. It is because our priorities are not aligned with the priorities of the globalists who claim to be better aware and better knowledgeable of the facts on the ground. They require us to be transparent but never allow us to check on their activities which are funded by our money. We have enough money for every need every American has. The only reason we are in debt is because we choose to pile up weapons, drones and military helicopters. Rich corporations believe they can bomb anything that gets in their way but that is simply not true and a psychotic fantasy to say the least. I mentioned how big the budget is for the Department of Defense. Would America really fall under Putin's control if we relocate some of those funds to funding day-care at the workplace or free college education?

It does not add up. Nothing can justify the situation but cruelty and oppression. In the brochures and letters I receive from the United Nations Refugee Agency I see pictures of Syrian and Iraqi children living in tents and camps marked "U.N.H.C.R." in blue that are within close proximity. They wear raggedy clothes and rely on whatever food the agency provides them with. To me that is no different than an abandoned newsstand being used as shelter by a homeless person in New Jersey. He relies on the soup kitchen and pantry. Both populations have been hurt by the same ideology and world view. The latter has been neglected so that the former can get hurt.

In my Comparative Politics class at Western Connecticut State University my professor once asked us "what is democracy?" The class was quiet for one minute. After passing two civics courses in high school, after making it to their third or fourth year in university, no one was able to define democracy. Now, had such a question been asked in for example, a class in Afghanistan it would have been clear why students would be silent. Finally, I raised my hand and mentioned the various rights like freedom of speech, freedom of religion and freedom of the press. Now that I think about that day I wish I had also added some other rights to my definition; like access to water, guaranteed education, stability and health care. After that incident my professor said she was going to make P.S. 100 a prerequisite for Comparative Politics.

We as a nation have a decision to make. Do we agree that housing, education and health are part of a democratic society? Are they requirements similar to the right to bear arms? If we do not believe these to be requirements for a democracy then we are fine where we are. We have more guns in this country than people. We have an unregulated press. If we do believe these are necessary for a democracy then we are surely missing a lot. Only when we come to this conclusion can we legally take steps to make work more family-friendly; add driver's education to our school system; make public transportation a common good and demand our government to fund Medicare and Medicaid.

"The Lexus and the Olive Tree" is over. We ignored its coming and we chose to ignore its leaving. It is time for new approaches and new opportunities. Libraries, public transportation, malls and schools can be places where all kinds of Americans meet again. We cannot afford segregation round II. We know the consequences of that. It is great to see various programs and settings dedicated to, for example, the disabled or single mothers. It provides an opportunity for them to connect and relate to people who share their same experiences, likes and dislikes and struggles. But we need to generalize and allow for more people to connect. Our lives are becoming too predictable. We do not have arranged marriages in this country and no one can tell us who to select as our partner in life so why are we choosing the wrong people? Why are we not proactive in where we meet?

I think we have a lot of which to be proud. There is no room to chastise ourselves. In fact, we could be more grateful and appreciative of some of the opportunities we have in this country. For example, it is completely unacceptable and inexcusable for us to have one million students abandon high school every year. Most of us are not required to work on our parents' farm and we don't have to fetch the water because we lack running water so why are we dropping out? Many students in poor countries dream of having paras and teacher's aides in the classroom to help them with their studies one on one. Most regions of the world still lack computers and access to the internet while others can only provide them through private education.

We could even be more grateful for the many freedoms we have. When I was reading about the Yellow Vest protests in France I could not help but feel proud for them. I thought it is no wonder the French lead the way when it comes to monitoring government. They are always on strike and even abandon work to go out and protest against something. The last time we had a major protest that could be comparable to the Yellow Vests was in 2008 during the Wall Street protests. Would we really call out a day to go out and make a stand? We fear losing our jobs even over some of the most basic rights like Family & Medical Leave or raising the minimum wage. Given the many freedoms we have and that they are backed by law or more formally the Constitution we should be out every day arguing against the criminal justice system; the never ending "war ons" and the health care system. Many came out once the election of Donald Trump became final in November 2016. The crowds were large and people from all walks of life were present protesting against the wall and the immigration ban. That definitely deserves credit but had we been out before the election of Trump; before the illegal occupation of Syria; before the defundings of our cities we would not have been confronted with a Donald Trump at all. Even after four years some Americans still believe Trump fell out from the sky. They completely ignore how we got here and what led up to his election. I think Trump has some points that we as Americans cannot ignore. It may be hard to put aside his racism and wealth for a minute to think about some of the major points he has made: media bias; never ending wars; fading traditions; wasting money; aging infrastructure and of course unelected officials or more correctly, wanna be actors, passing laws and making policies for the public.

Three of the global figures I personally admire are Mahatma Gandhi, Franklin Delano Roosevelt and Mikhail Gorbachev. Gandhi, for obvious reasons is our guide on how to protest against injustices of whatever form. He taught the world to stand up but make sure not to resemble the cruelty we are standing up against. F.D.R. led the country through the most difficult economic times America had ever had and signed policies that were so welcomed that no one could claim he was turning away from the global world. However, you might question Gorbachev. I think we have very rarely had anyone in history who was doing bad; hurting large populations; stealing from their own people; and fully committed to an ideology who eventually decided to put aside their views and power to come and say they did wrong. Gorbachev was Communist but he brought down the empire and was awarded a Nobel Peace Prize. He realized where Communist countries were headed and called for the dismantling of his own ideology. Whenever he met with other Communist leaders he would be disgusted or bored. Toward the end of the 1980s he left the leaders of Romania, Bulgaria and Hungary to fend for themselves. He ignored their calls for help in saving Communism. In America, we rarely credit Gorbachev for stepping back. We mostly praise President Reagan and congratulate him for standing up to a global threat. When Gorbachev was performing *glasnost* and *perestroika* our elites were demonizing him similar to how they demonize Assad, Maduro and Raul Castro today. They told Reagan to not take *glasnost* and *perestroika* seriously and keep on pushing the Soviet Union.

Donald Trump is one of the elites. He comes from the same ideology of neoliberalism and globalism. Yet since his election he has made neoliberalism very weak. He has dismantled some of the boldest points of the globalist agenda such as expansionism and the idea of the global village. He is backing down from his own ideology and crew and similar to Gorbachev he is hated by his club. When the Soviet Union fell, Gorbachev was discarded by the Communists. Few even know that he is still alive today and is 89 years old. I am not saying Trump is exactly Gorbachev. Gorbachev was not racist and definitely did not mingle with prostitutes. Trump does not deserve a Nobel Peace Prize. But he is a globalist and at the same time is coming out against his globalist views. He is dishonoring free trade, privatization, secularism and an open society; the ideals he is supposed to represent as a neoliberal. He has let down the satellite states: France, Germany, Britain, Canada, South Korea and Japan. What he still, however, believes in is the culture of cruelty. His views on women; people of African countries; Muslims; … comes from elite ideology. The same ideology prevalent in our police departments, army, prisons and the courts. The same ideology shared by the evil geniuses on Wall Street. The media likes to portray these as idiosyncratic to Trump; however, they directly support the very club Trump has come from. The club would like to hide their disgusting, dehumanizing and degrading views. However, Trump being the most honest president we have ever had openly states that he approves of all of Israel's invasions of Palestine; believes women are sex tools; thinks African countries are the last place anyone wants to be; and that oil is the main reason we attack other countries. President Bush never openly stated that he got involved in Iraq to steal the oil. He kept demonizing Saddam Hossein. He used the emotional trap to get Americans to feel something must be done. Obama also used the emotional trap to sneak into Syria, and Iraq round 2. But Trump does not consider where he is when he speaks. This has also let out a lot of other types of news about the globalists that they themselves do not want anyone to know such as the funding of the various terror groups. Trump has repeatedly said the young alienated men we hired throughout the West to overthrow President Assad are incompetent and unreliable. They did not get the job done and completely wasted our money. Trump let out the hypocrisy and culture of cruelty the elites have been profiting off of for 27 years. Neoliberals have constantly been looking for ways to overthrow him through a domestic coup yet we must see if he is able to fight them in the next election.

But we cannot go backwards and regret the past. We must save the connections now! We must refocus and defund fictional issues and the "war ons" whether there is a Republican, Democrat or neither of the traditional parties sitting in the Oval Office. Once we actually commit to doing that, we cannot measure our progress based on Gross Domestic Product, free trade or voter participation alone. These were the systems we used to measure our progress during globalization. We must find new ways of measurement like are we at war or peace?; how much new infrastructure have we built in the past ten years; and is domestic production flourishing or struggling?

Many countries have risen since the first Cold War. This is good and bad. China and East Asia is a pole. Iran is a pole. We caused this to happen. Had we not sent production over to Chinese factories would China have had the opportunity to open its doors? Never mind the fact that China is also a member of the United Nations Security Council. Had we not have overthrown Saddam Hossein in Iraq would Iran have had the opportunity to export Shiaism? Iran is the main reason for the fall of ISIS. Next to that we also must set up new institutions or reform current institutions like our Congress and our Judicial branch as I explained in "Our 'Victim' Justice System." We cannot afford to have our votes be ignored by lobbying. That is why I would ban lobbying altogether after this era. Had lobbying not existed would we have had $4 billion to prop up the prison industry? Most of us have probably not heard of the Non-Aligned Movement. However, this organization has been invested in a lot by developing countries. It has been used as a new form of institution to tackle capitalist expansionism and raise up countries that have traditionally been dominated by colonial powers. Many of its members are in fact some of the countries where the globalist ideology has failed to perform such as Iran, Syria, Venezuela and Bolivia. It is not just a group of underdeveloped countries anymore for major economies like India and South Africa have joined. Although China is not present, it is a major ally of the member countries. If the NAM does become a challenge we should not be surprised.

Symbol of the NAM in 2012 Tehran session

There is a Persian quote that says, "Whenever you catch the fish from the water it is always fresh."

# REFERENCES

Ali, S. (2013) "Which Country Spends Most on Video Games". *Countries Now.* Web.

Battaglia, N. (2012) "The Casey Anthony Trial and Wrongful Exonerations: How Trial by Media Cases Diminish Public Confidence in the Criminal Justice System". *Southern New Hampshire University.* Web.

Banerjee, A. & Duflo, E. (2011) "Poor Economics: A Radical Rethinking of the Way to Fight Global Poverty. *Public Affairs.* Print.

Barkun, M. (2011) "Chasing Phantoms". *University of North Carolina Press.* Print.

Boswell, J. & Parry, R. (2019) "El Paso Walmart Mass Shooter Patrick Crusius's Father Admits to Nearly 40 Years of Drug Addiction Which Tore Apart His Family and Claims He Has Spoken Directly to Jesus". *Daily Mail.* Web.

Cochrane, E. & Davis, J. (2019) "Senate Approves $4.6 Billion Bill for Border with Fewer Restrictions". *The New York Times.* Web.

Deresiewicz, W. (2014) "Excellent Sheep". *Free Press.* Print.

Dearden, L. (2016) "ISIS: Islam is not Strongest Factor Behind Foreign Fighters Joining Extremist Groups in Syria & Iraq- Report". *The Independent.* Web.

Economic Policy Institute. (2016) "The Cost of Child Care in Alabama". Web.

Gardiner, C. (N.A.) "How Educated Should Police Be?". *National Police Foundation.* Web.

Goldman, A., Schmidt, M. & Mazzetti, M. (2017) "Behind the Sudden Death of a $1 Billion Secret C.I.A. War in Syria". *The New York Times.* Web.

Griffin, A. & Kovner, J. (2013) "A Life of Instability". *The Hartford Courant.* Print.

History. (2018, June 18) "How the U.S. Supreme Court Decided the Presidential Election of 2000 | History". https://www.youtube.com/watch?v=D-nR_hmS6V0

Jordan, M. (2017) "Citizenship Applications in the U.S. Surge as Immigration Talk Toughens". *The New York Times.* Web.

June, D. (2005) "World Suicide Rates by Country". *The Washington Post.* Web.

King, B. (2019) "War Flower". *Potomac Books.* Print.

Milanovic, B. (2019) "Capitalism, Alone". *Harvard University Press.* Print.

N.A. (2020) "Men's Ranking". *FIFA.* Web.

N.A. (N.A.) "Timothy McVeigh". *Sun Signs.* Web.

N.A. (2016) "Global Health Observatory Data". *World Health Organization.* Web.

N.A. (2011) "Dropout Rates". *National Center for Educational Statistics.* Web.

N.A. (2011) "Homeless Statistics by State". *United States Interagency Council on Homelessness.* Web.

N.A. (N.A.) "Certified Nurse Aid". *Naugatuck Valley Community College.* Web.

N.A. (N.A.) "Aviation Science Management". *Naugatuck Valley Community College.* Web.

N.A. (2017) "Portugal Poverty Rate 2003-2020". *Macrotrends.* Web.

N.A. (2017) "Portugal Crime Rate & Statistics 1990-2020". *Macrotrends*. Web.

N.A. (2016) "Portugal Smoking Rate 2000-2020". *Macrotrends*. Web.

N.A. (2016) "Tattered Robes: The State of the Ku Klux Klan in the United States". *ADL*. Web.

N.A. (2019) "Quick Facts New Haven City Connecticut". *United States Census Bureau*. Web.

N.A. (2020) "Unemployment Rate in New Haven County, Connecticut". *FRED Economic Data*. Web.

N.A. (2018) "Yale University Undergraduate Geographic Diversity Breakdown". *College Factual*. Web.

Platt, T. (2019) "Beyond These Walls". *Saint Martin's Press*. Print.

Steves, R., & Back Door Productions. (2009). *Rick Steves' lectures & the Rick Steves tour experience*. Edmonds, WA: Back Door Productions.

Sebestyen, V. (2009) "Revolution 1989: The Fall of the Soviet Empire". *George Weidenfeld & Nicolson Ltd*.

TED. (2015, July 9) "Everything You Think You Know About Addiction is Wrong |Johann Hari". https://youtu.be/PY9DcIMGxMs

Trillium Direct Connect. (2019, May 14) "R.I. Interview with Peer Support Specialist". https://youtu.be/heVxiFKKRhI

The Grayzone. (2019, March 19) "Max Blumenthal Debunks Corporate Media Lies About Venezuela at United Nations".

United Nations. (N.A.) "Protection of Civilians Mandate". *United Nations Peacekeeping*. Web.

Webb, J. (2016) "Women are Still Paid Less than Men-Even in the Same Job". *Forbes*. Web.

Zavis, A. (2017) "Chelsea Manning Leaves Prison After Serving 7 Years for Handing U.S. Secrets to Wikileaks". *Los Angeles Times.* Web.

Zunes, S. (2016) "The U.S. Role in the Honduras Coup and Subsequent Violence". *The Huffington Post.* Web.

# ABOUT THE AUTHOR

ayla Faridani is a Master's degree student at Southern New Hampshire University. One of her primary areas of concern is the impacts of globalism on Western and non-Western nations alike. While the effects differ, Faridani asserts that both groups are suffering. She has been socially active in various public and private institutions for the past three years.